A Clean Heart

By Cheri Dedman

Copyright © 2007 Cheri Dedman
All rights reserved.

ISBN: 143920246X
ISBN-13: 9781439202463

Printed March 2007

All rights reserved.
No part of this publication may be reproduced or transmitted in any form or by any means without permission of the author. *(Appendix B CROSS - 53; Appendix B continued – 54 may be photocopied)*

Scripture taken from the Holy Bible, New International Version(NIV)

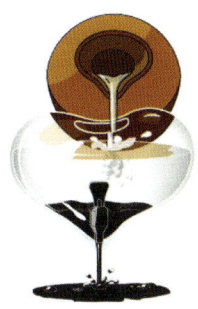

A Clean Heart

Is a deep Heart Cleansing, which is an intensive time of prayer, allowing the Father access to old hurts and wounds of the heart.

This is a proactive Bible Study that goes a step further than teaching about the effects of strongholds.

2 Corinthians 10:4
The weapons we fight with are not the weapons of the world. On the contrary, they have divine power to demolish strongholds.

By
Cheri Dedman

Table of Contents

Preface vii

Group Covenant ix

Foreword... xi

Acknowledgments.. xiii

Chapter 1 1
   Creation: God Created Us with Seven Needs

Chapter 2 11
   The Demonic Forces in Strongholds

Chapter 3 15
   Defining, Identifying, and Healing Strongholds

Chapter 4 19
   How Adam's Fall into Sin has Harmed Us

Chapter 5 25
   Steps To Identify and Demolish Strongholds
   The Obstacle of Pride 25
   Overview of Types of Strongholds 27

Step One 29
   Identify Strongholds Through Their Symptoms

Step Two 39
   Renounce the Strongholds

Step Three 41
   Cross/essing Thoughts, Feelings, and Attitudes with Writing and Prayer

Appendix 49

Preface

Dear Sisters in Christ,

Only by God's grace and mercy have I come to know liberty in Christ. I have experienced some life changing events in the past few years. I have been greatly humbled by these experiences. From the sincerest part of my heart, I wish to share this life changing truth with you. It is truth that has set me free (John 8:32). A yoke of bondage had become such a part of my life that the enemy had convinced me that it was just the way my life would always be. If all this sounds familiar to you, maybe God has purposed you at this time to go through **A Clean Heart**.

Oh, sisters, The Holy Spirit calls us by name and woos us to run into the Secret place of the Most High to abide under the shadow of the Almighty (Psalm 91:1). He truly is the lover of your soul!

The strongholds in my life, some of which kept me bound since early childhood, had set themselves up as a seeming self-protection from hurts and unmet needs. I refused to let myself become vulnerable to these hurtful experiences ever again. Little did I know that the walls around me were keeping God out. The enemy convinced me that "No one will ever understand. All the old, suppressed wounds must be kept secret." Hiding only intensified the pain. When held in darkness, they became bigger and bigger. But when exposed to the Light of Truth, Satan lost his power! As the Lord began to peel away the layers of my seemingly protective wall, He exposed the false belief of the enemy to His wonderful light. The Lord has tendered my heart and called me to share this with women who are experiencing similar circumstances.

A Clean Heart is a teaching from the Word of God on strongholds and the effect they have on our relationship with the Lord. It goes a step further than just teaching about them. We proactively go through a **Deep Heart Cleansing,** which is an intensive time of prayer, allowing the Father access to those old hurts and wounds of the heart. *"I have exchanged a heart of stone for a heart of flesh. (circumcised heart; Ezekiel 11:19).* Repentance and forgiveness is the key that unlocks resentment in the heart. (*1 John 1:9, Ephesians 4:32, Colossians. 3:13*). If we allow resentments to lodge in the heart, we begin to rationalize and suppress them (*Hebrews 3:12-15*).

A Clean Heart contains very personal issues in the strongholds' survey. Confidentiality and sensitivity are essential for all who participate. The last section is the **Deep Heart Cleansing Prayer** to give the Father full access to your whole heart.

My prayer for you is that God would have full access to all areas of your heart and could then pour His love into your new tendered heart.

Love in Christ,

Cheri Dedman

Group Covenant

A covenant is a promise made to each other in the presence of God. Its purpose is to create a safe environment of warm acceptance and trusted confidentiality. Women can open up and share their deepest hurts, needs, and mistakes with each other. Rick Warren, in his book <u>The Purpose Driven Life</u> urges small groups to make a group covenant including the nine characteristics of biblical fellowship listed below. * Appendix E, 1.

We will: *Share our true feelings (authenticity)*

Encourage each other (sympathy)

Forgive each other (mercy)

Speak the truth in love (honesty)

Admit our weaknesses (humility)

Respect our differences (courtesy)

No gossip (confidentiality)

Make this group a priority (frequency)

Pray for one another (intercession)

Date_____

Signature_____

Foreword

I think this book is awesome! There are wonderful truths and scriptural basis throughout the text, which is great. The whole area of strongholds and freedom in Christ is huge in our self-centered society-and the believer in Christ must know that truth and how it sets us free! I pray that God will bless this and open the doors He would have for you to go through to proclaim Freedom in Christ!!!

Jamie Wooten

I was saved when I was five years old. And, even though the Lord has never left me since that day, I have strayed from Him on more than one occasion. When I returned to my Father, I was hungry and on my knees. I was worshipping and attending a Bible study with fellow Christians, when I first met Cheri. She recognized my guilt and overwhelming desire to deepen my relationship with Christ. That's when I first learned of Heart Cleansing. When you combine the Spoken Word and Prayer, love and support of Christian friends and the guidance Cheri provides in "A Clean Heart," the power you will experience is immense. My life will never be the same. The strongholds of fear, guilt, manipulation, and others have been broken. Not only for me, but also for those I love and share my life with. I can only hope you will open your hearts and your mind to what this book reveals and know that the Lord will bless you for wanting a close intimate relationship with Him. "He took me; He drew me out of many waters. He delivered me from my strong enemy and from them, which hated me; for they were too strong for me. They prevented me in the day of my calamity; but the Lord was my stay. He brought me forth also into a large place; He delivered me because He delighted in me" Psalm 18:16-19.

Marnie Mitchell

Acknowledgments

Wow! Where do I begin? I could start at no better place than to say that the Lord Jesus Christ is my All in All! He's my Super Hero. I can't imagine where I'd be today with out His mighty outstretched arms that reached down and redeemed this wretched sinner.

It's only by God's grace that I'm here to tell about His wonderful love that is able to reach the deepest pit of despair. I was the worst of the worst. He saw fit to pull me out of that pit and put a new song in my heart. Life doesn't get any better. My Savior thrills me every day. I'm forever grateful for his attribute of Mercy.

I have so many people that I owe a huge debt of gratitude. My wonderful husband Stan, my sons, Stuart and Curtis: Guys, you are the men in my life that God so graciously blessed me with. I wish that I had known about how to be set free from strongholds sooner. I know that God will redeem the time that the locusts have eaten. How you put up with the pathetic mess I was is beyond me. I am so very proud of all three of you. Without a doubt you are men of integrity. I love you very much.

Robert Shelton is a man of God and stands firm on Gods Word. I'm grateful for his commitment to lead me through Robert McGees' study, **A Search For Significance** .******* Appendix E, 8. Finding out who I am in Christ has given me a new perspective in living out my Salvation.

Dick and Judy French of M.O.R.E. Ministry of Reconciliation & Encouragement are prayer warriors and humble servants of the Lord. They spent many hours with me in prayer and helped me to see that my bitterness and resentment were the enemy's biggest traps that kept me bound. They are in the business of restoring wounded Christians to the God of all restoration.

My heart has a special place for Dr. Joyce Wallace. She is an excellent Christian Psychologist and passionate in ministry to women of the Church body. She is so in-tune with the Father that from day one I knew that He would use her to peel my layers of pretense and get to the heart of the matter. Dr. Wallace was instrumental in leading me back to the heart of the Father. She is a vessel of honor that God flows through freely.

I have some awesome sisters in the Lord who keep me accountable, too many to list. We spend time together in the Word as well as Bible study and prayer.

There is no greater love than that of the Lord God Almighty. When I think that Jesus loves each of us with the same love that the Father has for the Son, I am amazed and humbled. Thank you Jesus for loving me that way. I'm forever grateful.

Chapter 1

Creation: God Created Us with Seven Needs (Genesis 1 and 2)

A study of the first two chapters of Genesis reveals that from the beginning God created in us **seven distinct needs**. *These needs provide continuing opportunities for His people to pursue a wholehearted and intimate relationship with Him as they depend on Him to meet their needs. As we seek to meet these needs* **within God's framework** *revealed in His Word, we provide the spiritual environment for an ever-increasing* **conformity to the image of Christ**. *As we yield our self-sufficiency to Him and focus instead on a God-dependency for all our needs, we will develop spiritual eyes to see His provisions and spiritual ears to hear Him say,* **"This is the way. Walk in it"** *(Isaiah 30:21). When we strive to meet these needs in a way that seems right to our mind, will, and emotions, but is not, in fact, God's way, we will suffer the consequences.*

God created us with seven needs:

1. Dignity
2. Authority
3. Blessing and Provision
4. Security
5. Purpose and Meaning
6. Freedom and Boundary
7. Intimate Love & Companionship

One source of strongholds in our lives is a result of seeking to meet one or more of these needs apart from God's will for us. Mike and Sue Dowgeiwicz *** Appendix E, 3

"And my God will meet all your needs according to his glorious riches in Christ Jesus" **(Philippians 4:19).**

Dignity

1. God Created Us with a Need for Dignity

"Then God said, 'Let us make man in our image, in our likeness,' …so God created man in his own image, in the image of God he created him; male and female he created them"(Genesis 1:26,27)

The dignity of being made in the image of God elevates us above all other forms of life in creation. Dignity encompasses our sense of honor, self-respect, and our personal distinctiveness. Satan assaults our dignity because we are **temples of the Holy Spirit** (see 1 Corinthians 3:16) and **members of Christ** (see 1 Corinthians 6:15). Our bodies in God's hands are **weapons of righteousness** (see 2 Corinthians 6:7).

Dignity is often eroded in families who use **guilt as a motivator** to control behavior. Phrases such as "You didn't come to see me yesterday, because I'm not important to you," or "if you loved me you would…." are manipulative and controlling. These words do not appeal to the dignity of the people or to his or her free will

Chapter 1

to act, but seek to **dominate by externally inflicted guilt**. *The loss of personal dignity prevents us from understanding who we really are. We fail to develop our own unique identity. Instead, many of our actions are controlled by* **what we perceive other people think of us or want from us.** *Self worth and respect are difficult to maintain in this type of captivity.*

> *As you examine your inner person, can you discern any ongoing area where your sense of dignity is being (or has been) violated, thus discoloring your sense of acceptance by God? Are you in the habit of violating the dignity of others?*

If your sense of dignity has been violated, you may respond to those around you through a stronghold of insecurity inhabited by a spirit of fear. Feelings of inadequacy and inferiority may cause you to develop relationships that could lead you into activities outside the will of God because you want so desperately to be accepted.

Authority

2. God Created Us with a Need for Authority

"And let them rule over the fish of the sea and the birds of the air, over the livestock, over all the earth, and over all the creatures that move along the ground"(Genesis 1:26).

The sense of authority and the understanding of authority have dramatic effects in our lives. Authority is the ***power of position***. It is the ***right to rule and influence***. The Bible tells us that authority was established by God for praise or punishment (see 1 Peter 2: 14). It also states in Romans 13:1,2, "The authorities that exist have been established by God. Consequently, **he who rebels against the authority is rebelling against what God has instituted, and those who do so will bring judgment on themselves**" (emphasis added).

Satan uses a misunderstanding of the biblical importance of authority to bring trouble on people. He knows that ***if we have trouble with authority, we have trouble with God.*** It is important for us to separate a person's authority ***position*** (i.e. father, mother, boss) from his or her ***personality and actions*** in that position. We should always give deference, that is, respectfully yield to the position of our authority person or intentionally limit our choices of action or decision so that we do not provoke that person. David showed deference to King Saul even though Saul tried repeatedly to kill him (see 1 Samuel 24:1-7). Jesus recognized in the

A Clean Heart

centurion such deference to authority that He could say about him, "I have not found anyone in Israel with such great faith" (see Matthew 8:5-13).

- *What response comes to mind when you think about the word "authority"? Is there a particular person your mind connects to that word? Can you think of anyone God has placed in authority over you against whom you consciously rebel?*

- *Are you a person who is equally as comfortable with "having authority" as with "being under authority"? Do you have a preference?*

*If you find that a stubborn self-will or a certain unteachability characterizes your response to the authority figures in your life, you may have built **a stronghold of rebellion** housing a spirit that is **influencing you to defy that individual**. You are unable to see God's good purposes intended for you by using these authorities to mold yielded submission into your character.*

Blessing and Provision

3. God Created Us with a Need for Blessing and Provision
"God blessed them and said to them, 'Be fruitful and increase in number; fill the earth and subdue it. Rule over the fish of the sea and the birds of the air and over every living creature that moves on the ground.'

Chapter 1

Then God said, 'I give you every seed-bearing plant on the face of the whole earth and every tree that has fruit with seed in it. They will be yours for food'"(Genesis 1:28,29).

God's character is behind blessing and provision. His name, Jehovah Jireh - **God the Provider** - is key to understanding the importance of trusting Him in this area. During your upbringing, if your real or perceived needs remained unmet, then your view of God as the Provider may have been hindered. "Did it ever occur to you that if you are prone to worry about finances, then God may bring you reason to worry just so you may learn to repent of it and trust Him? **Your worry insults His character** - Jehovah Jireh - God the Provider."

Proverbs 10:3 tells us, "The Lord does not let the righteous go hungry but he thwarts the craving of the wicked." **A stronghold of doubt and unbelief** may characterize this sphere of your relationship with God. Renewal of trust and belief comes only upon confession and repentance of these breaches of intimacy with Him. You must demolish the stronghold by renouncing the lying spirit and allowing the work of the Holy Spirit to be released.

- *On a scale of 1 to 10, where would you rate yourself in agreement with Paul's words: "I know what it is to be in need, and I know what it is to have plenty.* **I have learned the secret of being content** *in any and every situation, whether well fed or hungry, whether living in plenty or in want" (Philippians 4:12, emphasis added).*

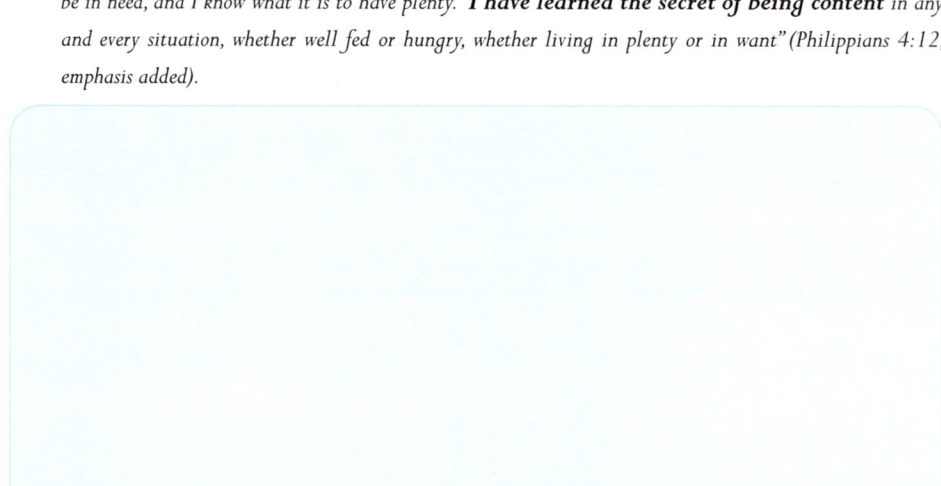

If you have difficulty finding contentment within the circumstances God has placed you or are fearful of a new direction to which He may be calling you (because you aren't sure the finances will be there), consider that **strongholds of fear and insecurity** *may be blocking this area of your life.*

Paul says, "I have learned to be content **whatever the circumstances**" (Philippians 4:11, emphasis added). He tells his spiritual son Timothy, "Godliness **with contentment** is great gain. For we brought nothing into the world, and we can take nothing out of it. But if we have food and clothing, we will be content with that. People who want to get rich fall into temptation and a trap and into many foolish and harmful desires that plunge men into ruin and destruction. For the love of money is a root of all kinds of evil. Some people, eager for money, have wandered from the faith and pierced themselves with many griefs" (1 Timothy 6:6-10, emphasis added).

Paul then concluded his discussion on money and the importance of trusting God: "Command those who are rich in this present world not to be arrogant nor to put their hope in wealth, which is so uncertain, but to **put their hope in God**, who richly provides us with everything for our enjoyment. Command them to **do good, to be rich in good deeds, and to be generous and willing to share**. In this way they will lay up treasure for themselves as a firm foundation for the coming age, so that they may take hold of the life that is truly life" (1 Timothy 6:17-19, emphasis added).

Give yourself a "contentment check": Have the besetting anxieties that plague you been due to your own foolish attempts to please yourself and your family **outside of God's will for you**? Have the pressures of peer comparison, pride of life, and lust of the eyes blinded you to the **peace and acceptance with joy** that contentment with God's provision brings?

Security

4. God Created Us with a Need for Security

"Now the Lord God had planted a garden in the east, in Eden; and there he put the man he had formed. And the Lord God made all kinds of trees grow out of the ground - trees that were pleasing to the eye and good for food. In the middle of the garden were the tree of life and the tree of the knowledge of good and evil. (Genesis 2:8,9).

Security may be defined as the condition in which we have confidence that we will experience **protection and relational warmth**. Spirits of **insecurity, rejection, and fear** oppress those who have grown up in homes with addictive or compulsive behavior or where some unexpected catastrophe occurred, such as the premature loss of a loved one or the sudden loss of financial security.

The absence of security leaves people in a prison, a concentration camp if you will, for years. They never seem to be able to draw close to other people in such a way that they feel like they "belong." Even in their relationship with God they never feel like He can accept them unless they are "doing something for Him." These people often hide behind conscientious behavior. They are viewed as the "reliable" ones we can trust to complete the tasks. What most are unaware of is that these people are often "driven" by the **need to be accepted or to be successful**. There is normally a tremendous "fear of failure" behind their actions.

- *Can you name three people to whom you would turn in a time of desperate need? Please list them. Have you actually turned to them? When was the last time you did?*

Part of the dimension of belonging to the "body" of Christ includes **intimate interaction and relationship with other body members**. God has not called us to be "lone Ranger" Christians!

Chapter 1

- List all of the activities, committees, or organizations in which you are involved. Circle the ones you **know** God has called you to do. Underline the ones in which you are involved for **other motives**. Are you feeling time-pressured?

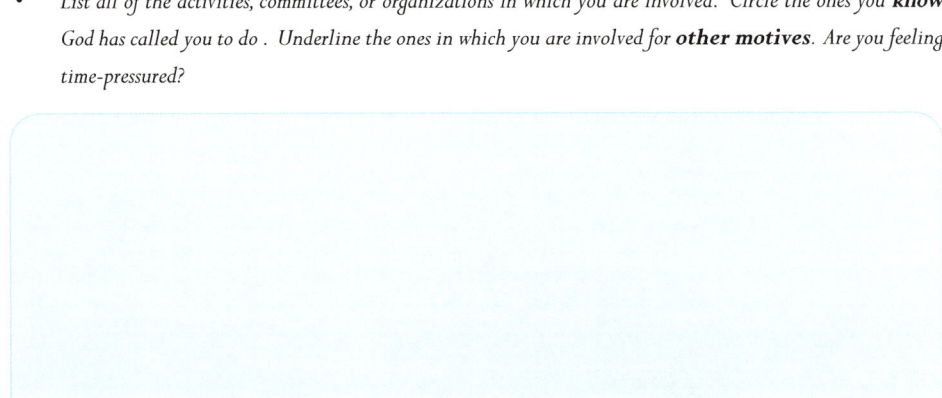

Once you see on paper the number of activities in which you are involved, you can begin to understand why time seems so elusive and fleeting. If you dig deeper into your soul, you might find that there is **a need you have been trying to fill by so much involvement What is the need?**.

Purpose and Meaning

5. God Created Us with a Need for Purpose and Meaning

"The Lord God took the man and put him in the Garden of Eden to work it and take care of it. ...Now the Lord God had formed out of the ground all the beasts of the field and all the birds of the air. He brought them to the man to see what he would name them; and whatever the man called each living creature, that was its name"(Genesis 2:15,19).

God gave Adam work to do before the fall (yes, **before** the fall!) to endue him with purpose and meaning. The Hebrew word for work and worship is the same: avodah. The culture of the United States has been heavily influenced by the philosophy of the ancient Greeks who considered pleasure and self-achievement to be mankind's highest goal. The Bible represents the God-centered view of **man's highest goal**, which is captured in Deuteronomy 6:5 and repeated by our Lord Jesus Christ:"**Love the Lord your God** with all your heart and with all your soul and with all your mind and with all your strength"(Mark 12:30, emphasis added).

Paul repeats the essence of the greatest of commandments so that our purpose and meaning in life would serve God's will:"Whatever you do, **work at it with all your heart, as working for the Lord**, not for men, since you know that you will receive an inheritance from the Lord as a reward. It is the Lord Christ you are serving"(Colossians 3:23,24, emphasis added).

Many today have lost the joy of God's purpose and meaning for their lives. Shopping malls are full of people purchasing aimlessly - believing the lie that acquisitions will bring them joy. Many labor at jobs only for material gain; they fail to discern God's deeper purpose for giving them that particular job. In all our actions, we should agree with Paul's exhortation:"And whatever you do, whether in word or deed, do it all in the name of the Lord Jesus, giving thanks to God the Father through him"(Colossians 3:17). If we can't agree with this, we are lacking God's purpose and meaning for our lives.

A Clean Heart

- *Can you put into words from your heart what you truly believe is the purpose and meaning for your life at this point in time?*

Don't despair if you can't. Recognize that God does have a significant purpose for you in His Kingdom, in order for you to bear much fruit and show yourself to be His disciple, to His Father's glory. (See John 15:8.) There may be some spiritual stronghold that is preventing you from discerning it. This is an opportunity for a few close friends to pray and fast with you, to discover both the blockage and the purpose.

- *What level of satisfaction are you finding in what you are doing at home? At work? In your faith community? In your world at large?*

*Consider the fruit of the Holy Spirit - love, joy, peace, patience, kindness, goodness, faithfulness, gentleness, and self-control - as **evidence** that you have indeed discovered God's purpose and meaning for you at this time in your life!*

Freedom and Boundaries

6. God Created Us with a Need for Freedom and Boundary

"And the Lord God commanded the man, 'You are free to eat from any free in the garden; but you must not eat from the tree of the knowledge of good and evil, for when you eat of it you will surely die'" (Genesis 2:16,17).

Chapter 1

*God loved Adam and Eve; He gave them freedom and boundaries **because He loved them**. We in North America have come to perceive any restraint upon our personal freedom as something negative. Many Americans consider people to be basically good, yet the Bible presents a different view concerning the basic nature of man:"The Lord saw how great man's wickedness on the earth had become, and that every inclination of the thoughts of his heart was **only evil all the time**"(Genesis 6:5, emphasis added).*

The Lord Jesus confirmed the nature of the inner man:"But the things that come out of the mouth come from the heart, and these make man 'unclean'. For out of the heart come evil thoughts, murder, adultery, sexual immorality, theft, false testimony, slander. These are what make a man 'unclean'"(Matthew 15:18-20).

*Because the basic nature of man is to do evil, the Bible tells parents to **"Impress them** [the commands of God] on your children. **Talk about them** when you sit at home and when you walk along the road, when you lie down and when you get up"(Deuteronomy 6:7, emphasis added). "He who spares the rod hates his son, but he who loves him is **careful to discipline him**." (Proverbs 13:24, emphasis added). "Folly is bound up in the heart of a child, but the **rod of discipline** will drive it far from him"(Proverbs 22:15, emphasis added). We have been created with a need for the **boundaries that God has established in His Word**. Failure to be diligent in having His commandments instilled in our children may cause them to probe the arena of sin to seek fulfillment.*

- *Against what boundaries - restraints on your personal freedom - do you find yourself tempted to push a little too hard?*

*Ask yourself why you may be testing your limits. **Spirits of bitterness, control, or idolatry** could be influencing your desire to stray from God's will for you.*

Intimate Love and Companionship

7. God Created Us to Experience Intimate Love and Companionship

"The Lord God said, 'It is not good for the man to be alone. I will make a helper suitable for him'" (Genesis 2:18). "For Adam no suitable helper was found. So the Lord God caused the man to fall into a deep sleep; and while he was sleeping, he took one of the man's ribs and closed up the place with flesh. Then the Lord God made a woman from the rib he had taken out of the man, and he brought her to the man. The man said, 'this is now bone of my bones and flesh of my flesh; she shall be called "woman", for she was taken out of man.' For this reason a man will leave his father and mother and be united to his wife, and they will become one flesh. The man and his wife were both naked, and they felt no shame"(Genesis 2:20-25).

*People yearn for intimate love and companionship! Satan has exhibited such great triumph over us by robbing us of our ability to experience loving and intimate relationships **God's way**. Many marriages are hollow. Sexual relationships have been based more on the teachings of Hugh Hefner and other pornographers than on the beauty that Adam and Eve experienced in a God ordained relationship.*

*"Intimate love and companionship" implies the need to be **loved, understood, and accepted**. How many times is 1 Corinthians 13 read at weddings? Yet the fruit of love diminishes rather than grows over the years of the marriage.*

*The **stronghold of fear** and the accompanying symptoms that the spirit therein induces restricts our ability to love and to feel the love of others, including the love of God. As strongholds are demolished and the **presence of Jesus is** allowed to fill those areas of our soul, **love replaces fear**. "God is love. Whoever lives in love lives in God, and God in him. In this way, love is made complete among us so that we will have confidence on the Day of Judgment, because in this world we are like him. There is no fear in love. But perfect love drives out fear, because fear has to do with punishment. The one who fears is not made perfect in love" (1 John 4:16-18).*

*"As we seek love-in all the wrong places," Satan's servants deceive us into rationalizing that we **have a right** to loving companionship **outside of God's will**. Each failed relationship further diminishes our trust level, thus filling us with cynicism and hopelessness in this area of our lives.*

Consider this: Over 70 percent of all weddings in the U.S. are performed in church buildings - and nearly 50 percent of these end in divorce.

- *How would you describe your relationship with your spouse or most intimate friend(s)? Deepening steadily? Staying pretty much the same? Heading downhill?*

*As we grow in the **sacrificial love** that exemplifies a Christ-like character, our relationships also deepen and strengthen.*

Chapter 1

- *Describe a point in your life when you experienced a relationship that you wished would never change. What happened to change it?*

Our lives are not static. The dynamics of daily life cause circumstances and relationships to change for either better or worse. We must discern through the Holy Spirit how to respond to these changes.

Our life *is a pilgrimage, a journey during which changing circumstances force us to adapt.*

Our ability *to make those adaptations in the power of the Holy Spirit will determine the level of joy and peace we find in our relationship with God and others.*

Our victory *of walking in the fullness of Christ will not be achieved until we meet the needs God has created in us, in the manner that He prescribes.*

Chapter 2

The Demonic Forces in Strongholds

In the New Testament, those who are afflicted by evil spirits are often said to be "demon-possessed." The Greek word translated in these instances, **daimonizomenoi,** *is more literally rendered* **"demonized,"** *that is,* **afflicted or influenced in some degree by demons.** *The emphasis is more on* **degrees of influence** *than on total possession. The intensity of demonized varies, as seen in the deranged man from the region of the Gerasenes who was inhabited by a legion of evil spirits (see Mark 5:1-20); the young man thrown into convulsions by the spirit tormenting him (see Luke 9:38-43); the demonized man who cried out in the synagogue where Jesus was teaching, "What do you want with us, Jesus of Nazareth? Have you come to destroy us?" (See Luke 4:33-36); and the slave girl who had a spirit by which she predicted the future (see Acts 16:16).*

As believers in Christ, we have been marked by the seal of the Holy Spirit, "A deposit guaranteeing our inheritance until the redemption of those who are God's possession"(Ephesians 1:14). We are owned by God; yet to the extent in which we have **fellowship with demons** *(Greek koinonia in 1 Corinthians 10:20) we open ourselves to demonic influence and affliction* **by our choices to sin.**

The battlefield for believers exists in our **mind, will, and emotions** *- what we often refer to as the* **soul.** *It is here that we face our daily decisions of Spirit-controlled living or sin-influenced living: "Those who live according to the sinful nature have their* **minds set** *on what that nature desires; but those who live in accordance with the Spirit have their* **minds set** *on what the Spirit desires. The* **mind of sinful man** *is death, but the* **mind controlled by the Spirit** *is life and peace; the* **sinful mind** *is hostile to God. It does not submit to God's law, nor can it do so"(Romans 8:5-7, emphasis added).*

Note the following warnings given to BELIEVERS - because we ARE susceptible to demonic attack, these admonitions are absolutely necessary.

- *"Put on the full armor of God so that you can* **take your stand against the devil's schemes***"(Ephesians 6:11, emphasis added).*
- *"For* **our struggle** *is not against flesh and blood, but against the rulers, against the authorities, against the powers of this dark world and against the* **spiritual forces of evil** *in the heavenly realms"(Ephesians 6:12, emphasis added).*
- *"Be self-controlled and alert. Your enemy the devil prowls around like a roaring lion* **looking for someone to devour"** *(1 Peter 5:8, emphasis added).*
- *"He [Satan] was given power to* **make war against the saints** *and to conquer them"(Revelation 13:7, emphasis added).*
- *"The Spirit clearly says that in later times some will abandon the faith and* **follow deceiving spirits and things taught by demons***"(1 Timothy 4:1, emphasis added).*
- *"Those who oppose him [the Lord's servant] he must gently instruct, in the hope that God will grant them repentance leading them to a knowledge of the truth, and that they will come to their senses and* **escape from the trap of the devil***, who has* **taken them captive to do his will***"(2 Timothy 2:25-26, emphasis added).*
- *"But I am afraid that just as Eve was deceived by the serpent's cunning,* **your minds may somehow be led astray** *from your sincere and pure devotion to Christ"(2 Corinthians 11:3, emphasis added).*

The key to the destruction of strongholds is 2 Corinthians 10:3-6, *"For though we live in the world, we do not wage war as the world does. The weapons we fight with are not the weapons of the world. On the contrary, they have divine power to demolish strongholds. We demolish arguments and every pretension that sets itself up against the knowledge of God, and we take captive every thought to make it obedient to Christ.*

We can clearly see by these verses that we are indeed engaged in the **same manner of spiritual warfare** that Jesus and His disciples confronted. Both the Old and New Testaments are replete with references to **evil and unclean spirits** (Greek **pneuma** in the New Testament and Hebrew **ruach** in the Old Testament).

The decisions we make to give in to temptation open up a ***foothold for demonic influence.*** One-third of the angels sided with Satan in their rebellion against God and was cast down to the earth. While we do not know their exact number, we can surmise that there are significant quantities of them to wage war against believers. But as we will explore in the following chapters, our **weapons of warfare** in this daily struggle to choose righteousness rather than succumb to temptation are indeed "mighty through God to the pulling down of strongholds" (2 Corinthians 10:4, KJV).

The Bible tells us that we are comprised of body, soul, and spirit: "May God himself, the God of peace, sanctify you through and through. May your **whole spirit, soul and body** be kept blameless at the coming of our Lord Jesus Christ" (1 Thessalonians 5:23, emphasis added). The **body** is the part that is subject to the physical frailties of injury, disease, and ultimately death. The **soul** consists of our mind, will, and emotions - the arenas of thought, determination, and feelings. The **spirit** represents the eternal part of our being owned either by Satan as the ruler of this world's system, or by God, Who has redeemed us from slavery to sin. The spiritual world is hidden from our vision, but nonetheless is **very real**. As believers we are encouraged by the assurance that our "spirits are seated with Christ in the heavenly realms" (Ephesians 2:6), and sealed with the indwelling Holy Spirit during our earthly pilgrimage. (See Ephesians 1:13)

In the spiritual realm there is a tremendous battle going on for the souls of men. In effect, it is a battle of God versus Satan. Its outcome will determine whether the truth of Jesus and His Lordship will reign or the deception of Satan will triumph. [NOTE: The overwhelming evidence in the Bible shows that God's plan for our lives is to **conform us in character and power to the image of Jesus Christ.**]

According to pollster George Barna, almost half of today's Christians **discredit the reality of the "devil"** in the person of Satan. His hatred for those who love God means that we are exposed to constant conflict and temptation. **We must be on alert!**

What can you know about Satan from the following verses?

- **He is the Ruler of the Kingdom of the Air, Now at Work in Those Who Disobey God**
  "As for you, you were dead in your transgressions and sins, in which you used to live when you followed the ways of this world and of the ruler of the kingdom of the air, the spirit who is now at work in those who are disobedient" (Ephesians 2:1,2).

- **He Masquerades as an Angel of Light**
  "And no wonder, for Satan himself masquerades as an angel of light. It is not surprising, then, if his servants masquerade as servants of righteousness" (2 Corinthians 11:14,15).

- *He Takes People Captive to do His Will*
  "That they will come to their senses and escape the trap of the devil, who has taken them captive to do his will" (2 Timothy 2:26).

What can you know from the following verses about the battle going on over the souls of men?

- *We Are Not Fighting a Habit, a Character Weakness, or Even Other People*
  "For our struggle is not against flesh and blood, but against the rulers, against the authorities, against the powers of this dark world and against the spiritual forces of evil in the heavenly realms" (Ephesians 6:12).
- *Satan is Committed to Our Destruction*
  Then the dragon [earlier described as Satan in Rev. 12:9] was enraged at the woman and went off to make war against the rest of her offspring - those who obey God's commandments and hold to the testimony of Jesus" (Revelation 12:17).
- *Jesus Came to Destroy the Work of Satan in Every Believer's Life*
  "He who does what is sinful is of the devil, because the devil has been sinning from the beginning. The reason the Son of God appeared was to destroy the devil's work" (1 John 3:8).
- *Satan Is Always at Work*
  "Be self-controlled and alert. Your enemy the devil prowls around like a roaring lion looking for someone to devour" (1 Peter 5:8).

Satan's influence in our lives is often hidden, controlled through **strongholds** in our soul - our mind, will, and emotions. (NOTE: In the Old Testament, the Hebrew word for "stronghold" is often used in a positive way to denote a fortification or defender for protection, as in 2 Samuel 22:3, "He is my **stronghold**, my refuge and my Savior" and Psalm 144:2, "He is my loving God and my fortress, my **stronghold** and my deliverer." In the New Testament, however, a very different negative connotation of the "fortress" idea appears. The enemy is not kept out. The spirits of darkness have been given permission **by my sinful decisions** to take up residence within those areas of my soul **not yielded fully to Christ**. The freedom available to me in Christ is denied and I am kept imprisoned by the influence of those spirits.

Chapter 3

Defining, Identifying & Healing Strongholds

2 Corinthians 10:4—For the weapons of our warfare are not physical, but they are mighty before God for the overthrow and destruction of strongholds. **5—The weapons we fight with are not the weapons of the world. On the contrary, they have divine power to demolish, strongholds. We demolish arguments and every pretension that sets itself up against the knowledge of God, and we take captive every thought to make it obedient to Christ** *(emphasis added).*

Colossians 3:8,9—But now put away and rid yourselves **completely** *of all these things, anger, rage, bad feeling toward others, curses, slander, foul-mouthed abuse and shameful utterances from your lips. Verse 9—Do not lie to one another, for you have stripped off the old (unregenerate) self with its evil practices. Verse 10—And having clothed yourselves with the new* **spiritual self** *which is ever in the process of being renewed and remolded into* **fuller and more perfect** *knowledge after the image (the likeness) of Him who created it. (emphasis added).*

A. What is a stronghold?

The original Greek word for stronghold is **ochuroma,** which means to fortify by holding safely. A stronghold is what one uses to fortify and defend a personal belief, idea or opinion against outside opposition. A self-erected stronghold will be seeming protection, from unmet needs, unhealed hurts, and unresolved issues in your life.**** Appendix E, 4.

Strongholds are sinful, self-protections, however they usually get us the thing we fear. They are mental, spiritual and emotional structures such as **bitterroot judgments, inner vows, lies and hearts of stone** that we unknowingly build protecting ourselves. Therefore the rewards of strongholds are seeming protection, power control, and security. However, they keep God out. They keep truth out. They become so much a part of us they seem like us. See-God's Lake of Blessing Appendix F. Page 57.** Appendix E, 2.

A stronghold keeps a Christian captive by anything that hinders the abundant and effective Spirit-filled life that God has planned for you. Anything not yielded to God is a stronghold.

B. The process of stronghold development

Strongholds are developed through demonic agitation. For example, reflect on some thought that you realize in your spirit is contrary to the mind of Christ, such as a sexual fantasy. At this point you have two options: 1) You can rebuke the spirit that put the thought there and think on those things that are "true, noble, right, pure, lovely, admirable, excellent or praiseworthy," as Paul recommends in Philippians 4:8. Or, 2) You can entertain that thought a little longer. At this point you begin to develop an emotion about that thought—lust, arousal, fantasy. As that emotion continues, you are moved to take some action, if not now, then at some ripe moment in the future. The seed of fantasy will eventually grow into an opportunity to fulfill that emotional longing and a sexual enactment may follow. If you choose to ignore the warning convictions of the Holy Spirit, you will continue in these actions until they become habitual. At that point, without God's power released in you by your repentance, you are then held prisoner to this habit by a spirit. A spiritual

Chapter 3

stronghold has been built in you. The "voice" of that spirit sounds just like your own inner voice; you don't detect its presence.

In Summary
1) Satanic-inspired thoughts are introduced into your mind.
2) Entertaining these thoughts bring on emotions.
3) Giving in to emotions eventually leads to taking some sort of actions.
4) Continual participation in this behavior causes you to develop a habit.
5) Once a habit is developed, a stronghold is built by that spirit.

C. How does God get shut out?

Since the "Spirit of him who raised Jesus from the dead is living in us"(Romans 8:11), we have the power to conform our minds to that of Jesus. We are able to make decisions that are pleasing to God according to the truth of His Word. The weapons we use to wage war against the forces of darkness have divine power to demolish strongholds. We demolish arguments and every pre-tension that sets itself up against the knowledge of God. (2 Corinthians 10:4,5). We can elect to put our feelings under the control of the Holy Spirit.

But since our souls are unfiltered by a stronghold, our mind, will and emotions filter all our perceptions through that demonic stronghold. This does not mean we are "demon-possessed"; we are demonized in those areas habitually given over to sin. As followers of Christ, we are inhabited by the Holy Spirit. However, those areas that we have willingly yielded to sin are fair game to become footholds for satanic involvement. We are warned in Luke 11:35,36, **"See to it, then, that the light within you is not darkness. Therefore, if your whole body is full of light and no part of it dark, it will be completely lighted as when the light of a lamp shines on you."**

D. Generational Strongholds

A major source of strongholds in people's lives come from past generations. Our Lord, jealous for His love, promises, "to show love to a thousand generations of those who love me and keep my commandments"(Exodus 20:6; see also 34:6,7), but to "punish the children for the sin of the fathers to the third and fourth generation of those who hate me"(Exodus 20:5). God desires that each generation love Him. The Hebrew word for love here is **ahav**, a devoted passion for the One you love, a strong desire to be in His presence. (See Deuteronomy 6:5; Matthew 22:37.)

When a generation fails to love Him or to repent of their sins, God chastises them and their successors to the fourth generation through demonic strongholds. When a generation receives light concerning their condition and repents and places their loving-trust in God, He mercifully forgives them. Nehemiah, Jeremiah, and Daniel knew the importance of asking forgiveness for the sins of prior generations.

"Let your ear be attentive and your eyes open to hear the prayer your servant is praying before you day and night for your servants, the people of Israel. I confess the sins we Israelites, including myself and my father's house, have committed against you"(Nehemiah, Jeremiah and Daniel are good examples.) "Be the one in your generation who will love our Father as He deserves so that He may be merciful to the future generations of your family. Humility is an ongoing need. Ask God to empower you with His Spirit so that you may love Him completely Fred Littauer . ****** App E, 6..

E. How do I break free from a stronghold?
1. Let God reveal it in all its glory. (Psalm 139:14-16, 23-24)
2. Expose roots, judgments and patterns.
3. Let Him probe the walls.
4. Develop an ongoing honesty of heart.
5. Admit helplessness.
6. Renounce it and invite God to destroy it.
7. Be willing to let God be your only defense. (Psalm 27:1-6)
8. Receive healing for the child like spirit inside.
9. Meditate and focus on the truth. (John 8:32.)
10. Practice new patterns of thought and behavior. (Romans 12:2)
    Paula Sandford ******* Appendix E, 7.

F. Thoughts to consider concerning strongholds.

Think of a situation in which you totally misperceived the motivation or intent of a person close to you. How did that misperception affect your relationship with that person?

*If you have never felt accepted or valued as a worthwhile individual, you might suspect that your friend was only trying to benefit herself. The **stronghold of rejection** may be manifested as a spirit arouses unwarranted suspicion or even withdrawal from your friend.*

How did you feel when you realized that you had wrongly interpreted that person's intent or actions?

*You may have felt tremendous guilt or a sense of unworthiness. The **stronghold of rejection** might cause you to believe that you don't deserve friends because you are such a poor one yourself.*

Chapter 3

How did you handle the relational breach? Did you find it difficult to humbly confess and ask forgiveness? Did you prefer to sweep it under the carpet as though nothing had happened? Did you feel pressure to rationalize and blame the other person?

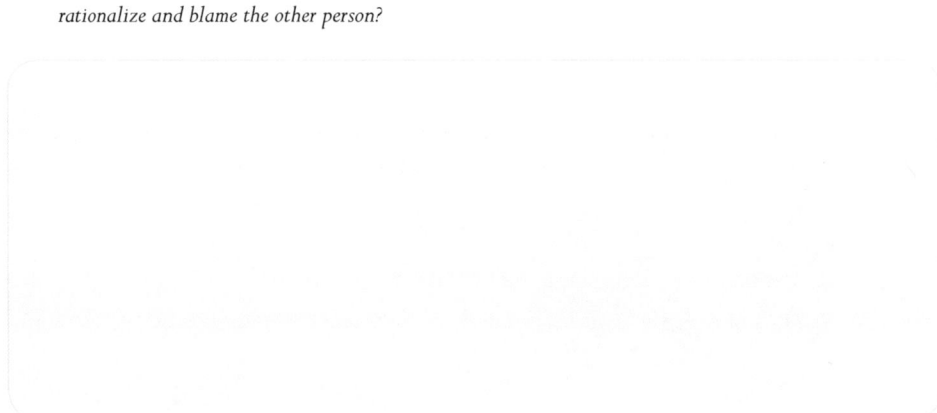

*The spirit in a **stronghold of rejection** could escalate your embarrassment and guilt to such an extent that it might prevent you from seeking forgiveness for your response.*

*Another example: What if the mental framework of your childhood focused on the memory that your father often disciplined you harshly? Every time you have thought about yourself and your father, you have had difficulty remembering happy times of togetherness because that one painful perception has filtered them out. Suppose you discovered that, in fact, the discipline situation actually occurred only once, but you were so humiliated by it that you then allowed the **lie** of "frequent disciplining" to replace the **truth** of "one severe disciplining? You may be "held captive" by the **spirits of bitterness and anger**.*
Robert McGee ******** Appendix E, 8.

Chapter 4

How Adam's fall into Sin Has Harmed Us (Genesis 3:1-4:7)

*The following examination of Genesis 3 provides a parallel of how Satan (the serpent) deceived Adam and Eve and, through demonic strongholds, **continues to deceive us today.***

A Stronghold

1. Harms Our Hearing From God

"Now the serpent was more crafty than any of the wild animals the Lord God had made. He said to the woman, '**Did God really say,** "You must not eat from any tree in the garden?" The woman said to the serpent, 'We may eat fruit from the trees in the garden, but God did say, "You must not eat fruit from the tree that is in the middle of the garden, and **you must not touch it**, or you will die""'(Genesis 3:1-3, emphasis added).

*If we allow our sinful thoughts to lead to habitual sinful actions that lay the foundation for strongholds in our souls, we lose connection with the Source of Truth. In the Greek language, **truth** and **reality** are the same word. The Lord affirmed the understanding that He was the only reality when He said: "I am the way and the truth [reality] and the life. No one comes to the Father except through me" (John 14:6). Anything that is **not** truth – **not of Jesus, therefore** – alters our reality into some sort of lie.*

- *Do you find yourself thinking that the Bible is "culturally entrapped" – that the timeless truths of God somehow don't apply to your current situation? What answer would you give to someone who presented that argument to you?*

Any time we try to rationalize an attitude or behavior that deviates from God's commands expressed in the Bible, we are opening a foothold for the enemy to plant seeds of distrust in the Author of the Word. It behooves us to become faithful students of the Word so that we might discern the life choices that will bring glory to God through us.

Chapter 4

- *How might a stronghold of insecurity affect your trust in the heavenly Father who has promised to meet all your needs according to His glorious riches in Christ Jesus? (See Philippians 4:19.)*

*God is infinitely creative in the means by which He keeps His promises. If we pray for specific answers to our problems, rather than presenting to God our petitions and requests with thanksgiving, we may not even recognize the provision from His hand when it appears. We may doubt He even heard us. In this way, **a stronghold will hinder our hearing from God.***

2. Harms our Belief in God

"You will not surely die," the serpent said to the woman. "For God knows that when you eat of it your eyes will be opened, and you will be like God, knowing good and evil." (Genesis 3:4,5, emphasis added).

The framework of our faith requires us to "trust in the Lord with all [our] heart and lean not on [our] own understanding" (Proverbs 3:5). We cannot view God as merely a repository of holy righteousness Who is independent of our earthly struggles. Our deceitful hearts are prone to make **Him** into **our image of Who we think He should be.** Sin causes us to doubt, or at least to hedge on, the reality of His character as revealed in His Word. Strongholds of **deception or doubt and unbelief** replace the truth with a rationalized slant that seems logical but leads to death. (See Proverbs 14:12.)

- *What areas of doubt or unbelief do you want to take up with God? For example, do the innocent suffer? Why haven't my unsaved relatives yielded to you? Why is it taking so long for my prayers to be answered? Something else?*

A Clean Heart

God is not obligated to explain Himself to His creation. Perhaps our finite understanding could not even grasp the purposes of Him Whose ways are not our ways and Whose thoughts far surpass our thoughts (see Isaiah 55:8,9). **A stronghold, therefore, taints what we believe about God.**

3. Harms Our Desires

"When the woman saw that the fruit of the tree was good for food and pleasing to the eye, and also **desirable for gaining wisdom**" *(Genesis 3:6, emphasis added).*

Have you learned to be content in whatever your circumstances? Dissatisfaction, comparison, and competition are all "horizontally focused"; that is, what our eyes see in other people our minds then want, if we have not learned to desire **only what God desires for us.** This "vertical parameter" – **limiting our desires to God's will and means of provision** – is His protection for us in that area of our hearts. When strongholds of **jealousy, insecurity and idolatry** hold us, we become distrusting of God's plans. We take matters into our own hands – agitated by the demonic spirits – and seek something we think is in our best interest but is not in God's plan for our lives. Our old nature, corrupted by its deceitful desires, again directs our will.

- *How might you rationalize an action or acquisition because it "seemed right" at the time? What instance can you recall in which you just went ahead and did something because you wanted to, without seeking God's plan first?*

There is much to be said for the counsel of your spouse or of a mentor whose life reflects faithfulness to God. Frequently they can see through your outward responses and explanations and probe your true motivations. These then can be held up to the Light of Christ for examination. **Unfortunately, strongholds distort your desires in opposition to God's will for you.**

4. Harms Our Actions

"She took some and ate it" (Genesis 3:6, emphasis added).

If you decide to dally with sinful thoughts, then sinful actions will result. If you refuse to submit to God and resist the devil, then he will be your companion in sin. A stronghold of **pride, idolatry, or sexual impurity** will influence you to pursue your own goal so wholeheartedly that any potentially negative outcomes are minimized in your mind. There are, however, **always-painful consequences** to sin. The pleasure of the moment is fleeting, and the subsequent guilt and regret further remove you from the intimate

Chapter 4

companionship you once enjoyed with God. *"But each one is tempted when, by his own evil desire, he is dragged away and enticed. Then, after desire has conceived, it gives birth to sin; and sin, when it is full-grown, gives birth to death"(James 1:14,15).*

- *What counsel would you give to a close friend who is contemplating an action that you now know violate God's will? How would you counsel that person if he or she were right in the middle of that sinful circumstance? After he or she has decided to try to stop the sinful behavior or attitude? Have you ever been involved in a circumstance like this when you knew you should speak up?*

Part of being your "brother's keeper" involves **risking the friendship for his good**, *especially if he is heading away from God and toward the enemy's territory. If you take a courageous yet loving stand for righteousness, your valor and words may help your friend* **recognize and defeat** *the stronghold that has been tempting him in sin.*

5. Harms Our Relationships with Others

"She also gave some to her husband, **who was with her, and he ate it***"(Genesis 3:6, emphasis added).*

There is good reason for the warning in Proverbs 1:10: *"My son, if sinners entice you, do not give into them."* A person considering sin is more likely to succumb to it if someone else joins in. We rationalize by saying, "What's **wrong** with it?"(Instead of, "What's **right** with it?"). Then we try to justify the sin by thinking that if it were really so bad others would not be doing it. Note that God is entirely out of the decision loop here. A **stronghold of deceit** influences us to believe that sinful actions may even strengthen our relationship.

- *Can you recall an instance when you were "sucked in" to a sinful activity at the request of someone you cared for? Did you realize at the time that you were violating God's standards?" Did that realization inhibit your participation in any way? How did you feel afterward? Did you sense any separation from God or loss of intimacy with Him?*

*We know from 1 John 1:9, "If we confess our sins, he is faithful and just and will forgive us our sins and purify us from all unrighteousness." Genuine confession of our sin will bring forgiveness and cleansing. However, we also have a **responsibility to those with whom we have sinned**. We need to humbly seek their forgiveness for joining in the sin, and make restitution wherever appropriate.*

When the fortresses of demonic influences – strongholds – have been built in our mind, will, and emotion;
> *HEARING from God is altered;*
> *BELIEF in God is shaken;*
> *DESIRES are distorted;*
> *ACTIONS are disobedient;*
> *RELATIONSHIPS are debased.* ******** *Appendix E, 4.*

Further Effects of Adam's Fall

Verse after verse reiterates the reality of our sinfulness: "There is no one righteous, not even one; there is no one who understands, no one who seeks God" (Romans 3:10,11); "For all have sinned and fall short of the glory of God" (Romans 3:23); I know that nothing good lives in me, that is, in my sinful nature. For I have the desire to do what is good, but I cannot carry it out" (Romans 7:18). If left alone in our sin natures, the **consequence will be death.**

As with our original parents in the Garden of Eden, we too have the opportunity to humble ourselves before God and confess with true repentance that through sin we have "missed the mark" of His holiness. The enemy, however, has a different plan. He activates his demonic forces to agitate us so that obedience to God's plan of forgiveness and cleansing is obscured in our minds.

Instead of receiving the forgiveness and restoration of the cross, we are tormented with the following.

1. **Shame** *(Condemnation)*
    "Then the eyes of both of them were opened, and **they realized they were naked**; so they sewed fig leaves together and made coverings for themselves" (Genesis 3:7, emphasis added).

2. **Rationalization** *(Hiding from God)*
    "Then the man and his wife heard the sound of the Lord God as he was walking in the garden in the cool of the day, and **they hid from the Lord God** among the trees of the garden. But the Lord God called to the man, 'where are you?'" (Genesis 3:8,9, emphasis added).

3. **Fear**
    "He answered, 'I heard you in the garden, and **I was afraid** because I was naked; so I hid'" (Genesis 3:10, emphasis added).

Chapter 4

4. ***Blame*** *(Inability to Take Responsibility for One's Actions)*
"And he said, 'Who told you that you were naked? Have you eaten from the tree that I commanded you not to eat from?' The man said, '**The woman you put here with me** — she gave me some fruit from the tree, and I ate it.' Then the Lord God said to the woman, 'What is this you have done?' The woman said, '**The serpent deceived me,** and I ate' (Genesis 3:11-13, emphasis added).

5. ***Curse instead of Blessing***
"To the woman he said, '**I will greatly increase your pains in childbearing**; with pain you will give birth to children. Your desire will be for your husband, and he will rule over you.' To Adam he said, 'because you listened to your wife and ate from the tree about which I commanded you, "You must not eat of it, "**Cursed is the ground** because of you; **through painful toil** you will eat of it all the days of your life. It will produce **thorns and thistles** for you, and you will eat the plants of the field. **By the sweat of your brow** you will eat your food until you return to the ground, since from it you were taken; for dust you are and to dust you will return'"(Genesis 3:16-19, emphasis added).

6. ***Rejection***
"The Lord God made garments of skin for Adam and His wife and clothed them. And the Lord God said, 'The man has now become like one of us, knowing good and evil. He must not be allowed to reach out his hand and take also from the tree of life and eat, and live forever.' **So the Lord God banished him from the Garden of Eden** to work the ground from which he had been taken. After he drove the man out, he placed on the east side of the Garden of Eden cherubim and a flaming sword flashing back and forth to guard the way to the tree of life" (Genesis 3:21-24, emphasis added).

7. ***Vulnerability to Satanic Attack***
"Then the Lord said to Cain, 'Why are you angry? Why is your face downcast? If you do what is right, will you not be accepted? But if you do not do what is right, **sin is crouching at your door; it desires to have you**, but you must master it'"(Genesis 4:6,7, emphasis added).

- *Which of these seven consequences of sin most often plague you? Do you find yourself afflicted by one or more of these effects of the fall even after you have confessed your sin to God? Why do you suppose this happens?*

If you do not deal with the underlying strongholds that distort your relationship with God, you will continue to expose yourself to the effects of the fall. Loving intimacy with the God of Holiness will seem out of reach to you.

Chapter 5

Steps To Identify And Demolish Strongholds

Recall that strongholds are built when you try to meet any of the seven basic needs that God created in you by ways that are contrary to His will. You end up wounded in the process. Once you determine the nature of a particular stronghold, you must **renounce that spirit's presence and influence** *in your life.*

You must still **discern the need that is lacking** *or unfulfilled and meet it in a way that God intended. It is important for you to be part of other caring relationships in the Body of Christ that can be used by God to meet these needs. Until this last step — meeting your needs within the will of God —is complete, you will be vulnerable to further stronghold formation.*

Members of the Body of Christ can be used by God to meet our seven needs in ways that He intended. Until we **meet our needs within the will of God**, *the potential for strongholds to form again is very great.*

Remember*: Once a stronghold is established, you provide a* ***"foothold"*** *for the devil (see Ephesians 4:27, a base of operations for the* ***"strongman"*** *(see Matthew 12:29). You then become vulnerable to* **demonic control, direction, influence and/or oppression** *(mild or heavy) in that area of your life. Not dealing with this stronghold can endanger further demonic activity and lead to the establishment of other strongholds with additional demonic oppression in other areas of your life.*

This chapter contains examples of strongholds ***(bold type)*** *on* ***page 26***.***. *Beneath each stronghold heading are listed related* **thoughts, feelings, or attitudes** *often produced by demonic agitation in order to sustain that stronghold. This list of strongholds shows the ones we have previously encountered.* **It does not represent an exhaustive list**. *God may reveal to you other strongholds and symptoms to which you have given ground. The related areas may be similar for certain strongholds, so use careful and sensitive discernment to identify the correct one. For example, one of the symptoms of the stronghold of* **bitterness** *is anger. The stronghold of* **rebellion** *also has the symptom of anger, but the type of anger noted here normally leads to arguments.*

The Obstacle of Pride

Taken from Breaking Free. Making Liberty in Christ a reality in Life. Page 58 & 59. By Beth Moore. ***** *Appendix E, 5.*

"I want nothing to hinder God's work in your personal life through these weeks. My convictions concerning this Bible study are bone-marrow deep. I know the reality of captivity and I know the reality of liberty. I will stop at nothing biblical to beg you to let freedom ring loudly in your life. Pride will be a huge inhibitor to the journey ahead."

Chapter 5

- ➢ *God wants to get to our hearts. Pride covers the heart.*
- ➢ *God wants to free us from any hindrances in our past. Pride refuses to take a fresh look back..*
- ➢ *God wants to treat us with the prescription of His Word. Pride doesn't like to be told what to do.*
- ➢ *God wants to set us completely free. Pride thinks he's free enough.*
- ➢ *God wants to bring us out of dark closets. Pride says secrets are nobody's business.*
- ➢ *God wants to help us with constraining problems. Pride denies there is a problem.*
- ➢ *God wants to make us strong in Him. Pride won't admit to weakness.*

We are on a journey to freedom. As we embark on our road trip, let's imagine that we have everything we need packed and ready to go: Bible, book, pen, anticipation, time set aside. But before we can take our first few steps, we run into a boulder on the road. The size of this boulder differs with each of us according to the degree to which we struggle with pride. I can hardly imagine that any of us see only a small pebble in our way. To go forward from here, God must empower each of us to roll the boulder of pride off our road to liberty. I believe this stone will roll if we give it three mighty shoves.

1. *The first shove is to view pride as a vicious enemy.*
2. *The second shove is to view humility as a friend.*
3. *The third and final shove is humbling ourselves before God.*

OVERVIEW OF TYPES OF STRONGHOLDS

DECEIT
Lying
Fantasies
Delusions
Rationalizations
Wrong Doctrine/Misuse
Of Scripture

BITTERNESS
Resentment
Racism
Unforgiveness
Anger/Hatred
Violence
Revenge

HEAVINESS
Depression
Despair
Self-Pity
Loneliness
Unconfessed Sin
Suidical thoughts

JEALOUSY
Spiteful
Gossip/Slander
Betrayal
Critical nature
Judgmental
Suspicious

CONFUSION (DOUBT & UNBELIEF
Suspicious
Apprehensive
Indecisive
Skeptical
Unsettled

REJECTION
Addictive Behavior
Compulsions
Seeks Acceptance
Unworthiness
Withdrawal

PRIDE
Vain
Self-Righteous
Self-Centered
Insensitive
Materialistic
Seeks Positions

RELIGIOSITY
Seeks Activities
No Spiritual-
Power
Spiritual Blind-
ness
Hypocritical

INDEPENDENCE & DIVORCE
Insensitive
Lonely/Aloof
Self-Determined
Devil's Advocate
Withdrawn
Excuse Making
"Martyr" Complex

STUPOR & PRAYERLESSNESS
Distanced from God
"sold" Love
Distracted
Spiritual Blindness
Laziness
Deceived

REBELLION
Self-Willed
Stubborn
Pouting
Strife
Factious
Divisive
Anger Leads to
Argument
Independent
Unteachable

FEAR & INSECURITY
Inferiority
Inadequacy
Timidity
Pleasing People,
not God
Lack of Trust/
Worry
Phobias
Perfectionism
Dread of Failure
Inability to Set
Goals
"Motor-Mouth"

CONTROL
Manipulative
Striving
Lacking Trust
Devil's advocate
Insensitive
Desiring recognition
Violent

SEXUAL IMPURITY
Lust
Seductiveness
Masturbation
Fornication
Adultery
Frigidity
Homosexuality
Pornography

IDOLATRY
Frustrated
Hopeless
Greedy/Selfish
Financial Problems
Wrong Goals/ Decisions
Living a Lie
Apathetic

TO RE-EMPHASIZE: **Strongholds** *are demonic forces at work* **influencing and controlling your soul** *(i.e. your mind, will, and emotions). The most common goal of all strongholds is to* **destroy relationships***. They not only block us from knowing and experiencing God's truth and love, but also prevent us from giving and receiving love, understanding, and having acceptance in other relationships. Because of the nature of marriage, couples are particularly susceptible to the effects of strongholds in their relationship.*

Chapter 5

Identify the Strongholds

Through my own experience, I have found it extremely valuable to work through, "Identifying the Strongholds" with someone you know well, and someone who knows you well. If you are married, ask your spouse to participate with you.

Experience has shown that most strongholds have been **passed along for generations** within families. The vast majority of troubled marriages have had the same prevailing strongholds **in both spouses**, and each spouse had received these from his or her respective parents. When the stronghold list was given out to churches, **most people in the church** had the same prevailing strongholds. In businesses, many of the **key employees** have identified the same predominant strongholds. In effect, it is not the people but the **spirits in the strongholds** controlling the goals, methods, and values of families, churches, and businesses. The symptoms may seem different on the surface, but the stronghold behind the symptoms is often the same.

The method I've found successful in identifying strongholds is to have family members or other significant person(s) check off the applicable symptoms under each stronghold that they think **pertain to you**. (This can be done to identify the strongholds that may be hidden from you.) Use a **scale from 1 to 10**, with 1 indicating low and 10 indicating high, next to each symptom to indicate the strength of its control, influence, or oppression within you. When others participate, you may want to have them indicate one number for you and a second number indicating the strength of the symptoms in themselves. Comparing and discussing the combined input can obtain a more reliable picture obtained as to the type and intensity of stronghold.

Do not be overwhelmed if you discover you have checked off a large number of strongholds. **God is not condemning you.** He wants you to demolish these spiritual forces by His power so that **your fellowship with Him may be fully restored.**

Refer to the following pages on **Identify Strongholds Through Their Symptoms** to determine which symptoms and strongholds are applicable to you. Before you continue, remind yourself that a stronghold is a "demonic fortress of influence" from which spirits function in the following ways.

- *Control, dictate, and influence your attitudes and behavior.*
- *Oppress and discourage you.*
- *Filter and color how you view or react to situations, circumstances, or people.*

As **you** desire to draw close to God, **He** will draw close to you. The words of Jeremiah are particularly applicable here: "'For I know the plans I have for you,' declares the Lord, 'plans to prosper you and not to harm you, plans to give you hope and future. Then you will call upon me and come and pray to me, and I will listen to you. You will seek me and find me when you seek me with all your heart. I will be found by you,' declares the Lord, 'and will bring you back from captivity'" (Jeremiah 29:11-14).

Step One

Identify Strongholds Through Their Symptoms

Instructions

- Examine the following specific strongholds. Consider if the verses listed describe your situation or condition.
- Identify any of the accompanying symptoms that may be present in your life. Ponder the definitions. (The Holy Spirit may bring other meanings to your mind too.)
- Use a scale of 1 to 10 beside each symptom. A stronghold is present when one or more of the symptoms have been habitually present in your life. (Your spouse, family members, or close friends may be helpful as you embark on this. Just ask them to refrain from accusation. Don't spend time denying what they suggest or trying to defend yourself!)
- I was so ready to be free from bondage that I listed strongholds with only one symptom or greater.

DECEIT

"If we claim to have fellowship with him yet walk in the darkness, we lie and do not live by the truth... If we claim to be without sin, we deceive ourselves and the truth is not in us"(1John 1:6,8). "The heart is deceitful above all things and beyond cure. Who can understand it?"(Jeremiah 19:9). "If anyone considers himself religious and yet does not keep a tight rein on his tongue, he deceives himself and his religion is worthless"(James 1:26).

It is best to deal with this stronghold first. Satan's initial interaction with mankind involved deception. Since your soul (mind, will, and emotion) is the battleground, you need **to see clearly** the nature of those areas you have yielded to the enemy.

Symptom:	Definition:
☐ Lying	Falsifying information with desire to deceive
☐ Fantasies	Fanciful thoughts that have little credibility
☐ Delusions	Deceiving self into believing lies; often used to cover painful experiences from the past
☐ Rationalizations	Reasoning with desire to gloss over problems; attempting to deal with serious problems superficially; making excuses to justify behavior
☐ Wrong Doctrine/ Misuse of Scripture	Reasoning a conclusion or position, then using the Bible to support the conclusion

Step One

BITTERNESS

"Do not let any unwholesome talk come out of your mouths, but only what is helpful for building others up according to their needs, that it may benefit those who listen. And do not grieve the Holy Spirit of God, with whom you were sealed for the day of redemption. Get rid of all bitterness, rage and anger, brawling and slander, along with every form of malice"(Ephesians 4:29-31). "Therefore I will not keep silent; I will speak out in the anguish of my spirit, I will complain in the bitterness of my soul"(Job 7:11).

The stronghold of bitterness may be present when you **habitually** feel one or more of the following symptoms when thinking of a particular person, place, or event. You may act kindly toward those who have no emotional involvement in you life but respond in defensive anger toward family or friends from whom you perceive an attack that isn't really there. Unforgiveness, in particular, puts you in a **prison of torment** (see Matthew 18:34,35) and brings pain to the one you have refused to forgive. According to Hebrews 12:15, a special problem with bitterness occurs: It **causes trouble** and **defiles the relationships** of others who are not even linked to the original painful event. For instance, unresolved bitterness toward parents often can show up later in a marriage and hinder bonding between the spouses.

Symptom:	Definition:
☐ Resentment	Continuous begrudging attitude toward someone
☐ Racism	Unjust narrow-mindedness; prejudice against whatever differs from your values or beliefs
☐ Unforgiveness	Inability to emotionally release someone
☐ Anger/Hatred	Feelings of wrath or rage; intense animosity
☐ Violence	Emotional outrage enacting physical abuse
☐ Revenge	Desire for retaliation

HEAVINESS

"How long, O Lord? Will you forget me forever? How long will you hide your face from me? How long must I wrestle with my thoughts and every day have sorrow in my heart? How long will my enemy triumph over me? Look on me and answer, O Lord my God. Give light to my eyes or I will sleep in death"(Psalm 13:1-3). "Among those nations you will find no repose, no resting place for the sole of your foot. There the Lord will give you an anxious mind, eyes weary with longing, and a despairing heart"(Deuteronomy 28:65).

We know from Scripture that God desires you to have a childlike faith in Him that trusts wholeheartedly and absolutely in His love and mercies. The spirit of heaviness convinces you that your condition is hopeless: that no one cares, that even if circumstances improve, it's only temporary and you'll be miserable again; your life is a cycle of sorrow and you can't seem to get off the downward spiral.

Symptom:	Definition:
☐ Depression	Feeling of sorrow, despondency, dejection
☐ Despair	An overwhelming lack of hope
☐ Self-Pity	A pattern of feeling sorry for yourself
☐ Loneliness	A sense of detachment of separation from others

- ☐ Un-confessed sin   Avoiding admission to God of known iniquity
- ☐ Suicidal Thoughts   A strong desire to end your life

JEALOUSY

"Then the Lord said to Cain, 'Why are you angry? Why is your face downcast? If you do what is right, will you not be accepted? But if you do not do what is right, sin is crouching at your door; it desires to have you, but you must master it'"(Genesis 4:6-7). "You are still worldly. For since there is jealousy and quarreling among you, are you not worldly?" (1 Corinthians 3:3). "Whenever one comes to see me, he speaks falsely, while his heart gathers slander; then he goes out and spreads it abroad"(Psalm 41:6).

Like Cain, when you focus on the behavior and attitudes of others, you can develop a **judgmental posture** toward them. Rather than regarding them more highly than yourself as Scripture exhorts and respecting them for their godliness, you may begin to actively seek out their "warts"; you keep attuned to bad reports about that individual. By comparison, you appear better in your own mind.

Symptom: *Definition:*
- ☐ Spiteful   Malicious attitude intending evil toward others
- ☐ Gossip / Slander   Pattern of sharing detrimental information about someone with those not part of the problem or solution; telling part of the truth with a desire to hurt
- ☐ Betrayal   Breaking faith and turning against others
- ☐ Critical Nature   Habitual pattern of fault-finding; never satisfied
- ☐ Judgmental   Feeling better about yourself by evaluating others in a way that predetermines their failure of some prescribed standard or criterion
- ☐ Suspicious   Pattern of disturbing and doubting the motives of others

CONFUSION / DOUBT and UNBELIEF

"If any of you lacks wisdom, he should ask God, who gives generously to all without finding fault, and it will be given to him. But when he asks, he must believe and not doubt, because he who doubts is like a wave of the sea, blown and tossed by the wind. That man should not think he will receive anything from the Lord; he is a double-minded man, unstable in all he does"(James 1:5-8). "Jesus replied, 'No one who puts his hand to the plow and looks back is fit for service in the kingdom of God': (Luke 9:62). "'Come,' he said. Then Peter got down out of the boat, and walked on the water and came to Jesus. But when he saw the wind, he was afraid and, beginning to sink, cried out, 'Lord, save me!' Immediately Jesus reached out his hand and caught him. 'You of little faith,'he said, 'why did you doubt?'" (Matthew 14:29-31).

If you have entered into your relationship with Jesus based on a faulty understanding of **Who He is**, you will be unable to grasp how high and wide and deep is His love for you. He is LORD, and as such desires **Lordship in your life**. If you are focusing more on the adverse circumstances in your life rather than on the One Who can free you, you are listening to the spirit of confusion. When you truly comprehend the enormity of your sin and the vastness of His atonement on your behalf, you can then persevere in the "arena of suffering"

Step One

that your earthly life calls for. Assured of His plan, you may be confident that His purpose and His presence will continue without fail.

Symptom:	Definition:
☐ Suspicious	Doubt or disbelief in God's promises
☐ Apprehensive	Anxiously fearful that God will not fulfill His plans for your good or that He "has it in for you"
☐ Indecisive	Intimate trust in Jesus is non-existent; double-minded anguish from indecision
☐ Skeptical	Continuous pattern of questioning and hesitancy to trust God
☐ Unsettled	Unable to experience fruit of the Spirit in your life

REJECTION

"He has alienated my brothers from me; my acquaintances are completely estranged from me. My kinsmen have gone away, my friends have forgotten me" (Job 19:13-14). "Scorn has broken my heart and has left me helpless; I looked for sympathy, but there was none, for comforters, but I found none" (Psalm 69:20).

*When you feel that you **really don't matter** to others, the inner pain can be crippling. To avoid having to face the pain, this spirit induces you to compensate by just **coping**: You might avoid those whom you feel might bring you distress; you might escape through chemical means to ease the pain; you might act without care or concern about how your actions may affect others around you; or you might try to do acts of kindness in a desperate attempt to "earn" love and acceptance.*

Symptom:	Definition:
☐ Addictive Behavior	Obsession, intense preoccupation; detrimental habits such as gluttony, alcoholism, drug abuse
☐ Compulsions	Irrational obsession to act without forethought or regard to outcome
☐ Seeking Acceptance	Acting in kindness and friendliness with underlying motive to forestall rejection
☐ Unworthiness	Feeling unacceptable or inferior; never feeling like you can ever "measure up"
☐ Withdrawal	Removing self emotionally or physically from real or perceived hurtful and rejecting situations

PRIDE

"By your great skill in trading you have increased your wealth, and because of your wealth your heart has grown proud" (Ezekiel 28:5). "I will break down your stubborn pride and make the sky above you like iron and the ground beneath you like bronze" (Leviticus 26:19). "There are those who curse their fathers and do not bless their mothers; those who are pure in their own eyes and yet are not cleansed of their filth; those whose eyes are ever so haughty, whose glances are so disdainful" (Proverbs 30:11-13).

*As a culture, Americans are obsessed with **image and appearance**. The focus on maintaining youthful health has surpassed stewardship of the body and has become an idol. We know more about fat grams than we do about the standards of holy living in Proverbs. The image we project through our homes, vehicles, attire,* and activities becomes the means to our personal sense of worth. We not only have no desire to emulate the life standards of our parents, we pretty much have disassociated ourselves with them, either geographically or socially. Because God gives grace to the humble, the spirit of pride influences a person to focus instead on **self-gratification and personal fulfillment.** In our desire to appear "Christian," we feel better about what we **don't do** that's "evil" than about the "good" that God wants to do in and through us.

Symptom: *Definition:*
- ☐ *Vain* — Conceited pretension about own importance
- ☐ *Self-Righteous* — High opinion of own moral position compared to that of others
- ☐ *Self-Centered* — Obsessive egocentric pattern of thinking; "the world revolves around me"
- ☐ *Insensitive* — Unaware of impact on others; a bull-in-a-china-shop atmosphere created
- ☐ *Materialistic* — Obsessive desire to acquire and hoard in order to gain recognition or prestige
- ☐ *Seeks Positions* — Viewing people and resources as means of fulfilling ego needs; relationships have no worth except to advance self.

RELIGIOSITY

"I know your deeds; you have a reputation of being alive, but you are dead. Wake up! Strengthen what remains and is about to die, for I have not found your deeds complete in the sight of my God. Remember, therefore, what you have received and heard; obey it, and repent" (Revelaton 3:1-3). "In the same way, on the outside you appear to people as righteous but on the inside you are full of hypocrisy and wickedness" (Matthew 23:28).

Maybe you have been a believer for many years, serving the needs of the kingdom even to the point of burnout. People you have ministered to have been strengthened and encouraged; yet your own walk with Jesus has become impersonal and shallow. You may be at the point of going through the motions with no sense of loving God with all your heart, soul, and strength. Because others have always seen you as a spiritual pillar of strength, you feel you must **maintain that facade**, even if your inward pain is unbearable.
****** *Appendix E, 6.*

Symptoms: *Definition:*
- ☐ *Seeks Activities* — Intimate relationship with Jesus is non-existent; underlying attitude that "I must earn God's love; He will only love and accept me if I keep busy for Him"
- ☐ *No Spiritual Power* — Presence of the nature, character, or power of Jesus Christ lacking even after many years of religious practice
- ☐ *Spiritual Blindness* — Unable to know the will of God or to receive guidance by His Spirit
- ☐ *Hypocritical* — Expressing truths and performing actions that may bless others but do not really emanate from your own life

INDEPENDENCE and DIVORCE

"The eye cannot say to the hand, 'I don't need you!' And the head cannot say to the feet, 'I don't need you!'" (1 Corinthians 12:21). "Plans fail for lack of counsel, but with many advisors they succeed" (Proverbs 15:22).

Step One

"They went out from us, but they did not really belong to us. For if they had belonged to us, they would have remained with us; but their going showed that none of them belonged to us" (1 John 2:19). "'For this reason a man will leave his father and mother and be united to his wife, and the two will become one flesh.' So they are no longer two, but one. Therefore what God has joined together, let man not separate" (Matthew 19:5-6).

When you disconnect from others (family members, neighbors, co-workers, fellow believers, schoolmates), you tend to rely on your own efforts for decision. **"He who trusts in himself is a fool, but he who walks in wisdom is kept safe." Proverbs 28:26** says what you really don't want to hear. While we may desperately wish that someone would make the effort to reach in past our abrasive or withdrawn demeanor, you aren't so sure that you want the responsibilities that come with relationship.

"Divorce" is not necessarily related to marriage. It can manifest itself in any interpersonal situations in which you walk away physically or emotionally due to real or perceived hurt. If you feel that **belonging to others is optional**, you then can justify why you can separate yourself from them. You are able to rationalize that it is easier (or more beneficial) for others if you simply leave rather than confront issues or sins that need to be addressed. Ultimately, the spirit of divorce leads to unforgiveness, bitterness, and guilt.

Symptom:	Definition:
☐ Insensitive	Unaware of impact on others; a bull-in-a-china shop atmosphere created
☐ Lonely / Aloof	Sense of detachment; unresponsive to others' needs
☐ Self-Determined	Relies solely on own analysis and appraisal for personal decisions
☐ Devil's Advocate	Takes contrary position in discussion; argues without considering others' feelings or needs
☐ Withdrawn	Removing self emotionally or physically from real or perceived hurtful and rejecting situations
☐ Excuse Making	Rationalizing with intent to blame other(s)
☐ Lack of Trust	Unable to rely / depend on others; underlying attitude, "If you hurt me or let me down, I'm gone." Places incredible pressure on relationship to never confront problems
☐ "Martyr complex"	Deceived sense that your leaving will actually benefit others, and that you won't be missed

STUPOR/PRAYERLESSNESS

"As it is written, 'God gave them a spirit of stupor, eyes so that they could not see and ears so that they could not hear, to this very day'" (Romans 11:8). "For day after day they seek me out; they seem eager to know my ways, as if they were a nation that does what is right and has not forsaken the commands of its God. They ask me for just decisions and seem eager for God to come near them" (Isaiah 58:2). "And do this, understanding the present time. The hour has come for you to wake up from your slumber, because our salvation is nearer now than when we first believed" (Romans 13:11).

Because you feel as though the Holy Spirit has not been revealing anything to your spirit, your expectations of Divine involvement and intervention are almost nil. You may have become so **wrapped up** in the cares and activities of life, that you don't spend much time seeking the Lord. You **fail to appreciate** the "little" blessings and kindnesses that God has been pouring out. Perhaps you are so desperate for one key *answer to prayer that you have disregarded His other activities all around you. You fail to see that God might be allowing various trials in your life to conform your character to Christ's; you would rather remain in the "comfort zone" as far as opportunities for deepening your faith are concerned.*

Symptom:	Definition:
☐ Distanced from God	God viewed as "unconcerned"; sense of hopelessness felt when presenting needs to Him; underlying thought of "If I pray, He won't answer."
☐ "Cold" Love	Prayer viewed as obligation of religious practice rather than communication with someone loved
☐ Distracted	Unable to focus on communication with God; thoughts and worries invade prayer
☐ Spiritual Blindness	Unable to know God's will or receive guidance by His Spirit
☐ Laziness	Resistant to industrious pursuit of God's plans for your life; "your walk doesn't match your talk"
☐ Deceived Self-Appraisal	Unable to detect personal sin that may be hindering your prayers

REBELLION

"There is no fear of God before his eyes. For in his own eyes he flatters himself too much to detect or hate his sin. The words of his mouth are wicked and deceitful; he has ceased to be wise and to do good" (Psalm 36:1-3). "But my people would not listen to me; Israel would not submit to me. So I gave them over to their stubborn hearts to follow their own devices" (Psalm 81:11,12).

*Rebellion festers privately in the heart of the person who is open to it, but ultimately shows its hand in a public way. Some strongholds remain hidden from interference in the lives of others, but the spirit of rebellion searches for others with whom to stir up dissension. The weapon wielded by this spirit is **the tongue** — "a fire, a world of evil among the parts of the body" (James 3:6). Rather than listening to others, a person influenced by a rebellious spirit pushes for his or her own way vocally and forcefully, unconcerned for the wounded relationships left in the wake.*

Symptom:	Definition:
☐ Self-Willed	Concerned with wanting own way more than the will of God or others in authority
☐ Stubborn	Obstinate attitude toward others and reluctance to accept truth or help from others
☐ Pouting	Visible sulking behavior, indicating rejection of a truth or situation
☐ Strife	Clashing; creating unnecessary conflict in relationships
☐ Factious	Joining together with other dissenting people with desire to conspire or plot
☐ Divisive	Encouraging disagreement rather than seeking points of agreement; often playing "devil's advocate"
☐ Anger Leads to Argument	Hostile feelings leading to arguments often disguised as desire to explain your position or build your case
☐ Independent	Maintaining self-reliant and separate position from others; unable to belong
☐ Unteachable	Continuing to return to same errant position; often mocking those trying to help

Step One

FEAR and INSECURITY

"Fear and trembling have beset me; horror has overwhelmed me. I said, 'Oh, that I had the wings of a dove! I would fly away and be at rest — I would flee far away and stay in the desert'" (Psalm 55:5-7). "Strengthen the feeble hands, steady the knees that give way; say to those with fearful hearts, 'Be strong, and do not fear'" (Isaiah 35:3,4). "What I feared has come upon me; what I dreaded has happened to me. I have no peace, no quietness; I have no rest, but only turmoil" (Job 3:25,26).

Do you wonder why you often think, **"If I don't do it, it won't get done right?"** *Maybe you are wrestling with what one writer has termed* **False Expectations Appearing Real.** *Perhaps you have projected your expectations of outcome onto others, causing them to feel anxious and pressured. You may be struggling with the heavy burden of responsibility to meet your perception of what constitutes "acceptable." The* **task** *seems much more important to you than the people you are with. If probed, you would be hard-pressed to come up with a reason why you are compelled to do rather than to be.*

There are times when anyone would much rather be somewhere else than in the middle of the situation that is producing sweats and heart palpitations. However, the spirit of fear **consistently convinces you** *that you have nothing worthwhile to contribute, that if you speak up no one will accept what you have to offer, and that people will just turn away from you. In effect, the hunger to please those around you surpasses your desire to obey what you know God wants you to do or say.*

Symptom: *Definition:*

☐ *Inferiority* — Feeling subordinate or lower than others

☐ *Inadequacy* — Feeling incompetent or inept in accomplishing things

☐ *Timidity* — Feelings of shyness, bashfulness, or cowardice; often leads to withdrawal from others

☐ *Pleasing people, not God* — Overly concerned about what others might think

☐ *Lack of trust / worry* — Never feeling comfortable, lacking a sense of "belonging" to others; may appear friendly but have few or no deep friendships

☐ *Phobias* — Obsessive fear, aversion to, or dislike of a particular person or situation, often with no apparent foundation

☐ *Perfectionist* — Obsessive desire for flawlessness; inability to find satisfaction

☐ *Dread of Failure* — Shame-based motivation with abnormal pressure to always succeed; you rely on self in times of pressure and fail to turn to or trust others

☐ *Inability to See Goals* — Prolonged pattern of indecisiveness; feel threatened by potential confrontation in decision making process

☐ *"Motor-Mouth"* — Constant chatter that precludes input from others

CONTROL

"For he says, 'By the strength of my hand I have done this, and by my wisdom, because I have understanding'" (Isaiah 10:13). "For by the grace given me I say to every one of you: Do not think of yourself more highly than you ought, but rather think of yourself with sober judgment, in accordance with the measure of faith God has given you" (Romans 12:3).

*You feel that your input and decisions are key. In fact, you really don't trust that anyone else can see the whole picture as clearly as you can. You are willing to shoulder the responsibility but recognize the need for assistance, particularly if the participants are willing to **follow your suggestions**. If others offer advice, you tend to doubt both their capability and their motives; you are driven even harder to achieve the desired goal.*

Symptom:	Definition:
☐ Manipulative	Desire to maneuver or orchestrate the lives of others for personal advantage
☐ Striving	Endeavoring and struggling to accomplish; difficult for you to just "be"
☐ Lacking Trust	Inability to rely on others or to have confidence in God
☐ Devil's Advocate	Takes contrary position in discussions; argues without considering others' feelings or needs
☐ Insensitive	Unaware of impact on others; a bull-in-a-china-shop atmosphere created around self
☐ Desiring Recognition	Seeking acclaim or notice for what you do
☐ Violent	Emotional outrage enacting physical abuse

SEXUAL IMPURITY

"[The Gentiles] are darkened in their understanding and separated from the life of God because of the ignorance that is in them due to the hardening of their hearts. Having lost all sensitivity, they have given themselves over to sensuality so as to indulge in every kind of impurity, with a continual lust for more" (Ephesians 4:18,19). "Let us behave decently, as in the daytime, not in orgies and drunkenness, not in sexual immorality and debauchery, not in dissension and jealousy"(Romans 13:13).

*Often sexual sin is done in the dark – figuratively and literally. A darkened understanding of God's standards of purity greatly decreases your sensitivity to the ever-increasing violations of those standards. The individual influenced by this spirit **throws off restraints** – first in the mind and then in the flesh. Gratification becomes the issue; the relationship becomes secondary. Even in regard to frigidity, the relationship has ceased to be the priority.*

"Do you not know that he who unites himself with a prostitute is one with her in body? For it is said, 'The two will become one flesh.' But he who unites himself with the Lord is one with him in spirit. Flee from sexual immorality. All other sins a man commits are outside his body, but he who sins sexually sins against his own body. Do you not know that your body is the temple of the Holy Spirit, who is in you, whom you have received form God? You are not your own; you were bought at a price. Therefore honor God with your body" (1 Corinthians 6:16-20).

When people have sexual relations outside of marriage, a "soul tie" develops between them and their partner because the two have become one. Soul ties create a barrier to the fulfillment of God's plan for love in marriage. The tie with each sexual partner must be renounced in the name of Jesus.

Step One

Symptom:	**Definitions:**
☐ Lust	Lecherous desire to sexually possess someone forbidden by God's law
☐ Seductiveness	Using sexual arousal to allure interest
☐ Masturbation	Personal gratification as opposed to self-control
☐ Fornication	Sexual relationships between unmarried people
☐ Adultery	Sexual desire and/or relationships by married person outside of marriage
☐ Frigidity	Inhibited, indifferent, passionless view toward sexual relations
☐ Homosexuality	Sexual relationship with member of same gender
☐ Pornography	Desire for vicarious sexual arousal

IDOLATRY

"People who want to get rich fall into temptation and a trap and into many foolish and harmful desires that plunge men into ruin and destruction. For the love of money is a root of all kinds of evil. Some people, eager for money, have wandered from the faith and pierced themselves with many griefs"(1 Timothy 6:9-10).

A rich man was once asked, "How much money is enough?" He replied, "A little bit more." To crave and yearn for more of earth's treasures and pleasures defy God's will to "seek first the kingdom." You are unable to be grateful for what you have because you are disconnected from the Source of peace. "Happiness" seems to be just out of grasp. You long with all your heart for whatever you think will bring contentment. That becomes your next idol.

Symptom:	**Definition:**
☐ Frustrated	Continuous feelings of perplexity; nothing seems to go right
☐ Hopeless	Strong feelings of depression and despondency
☐ Greedy/selfish	Stinginess or excessive self-indulgence
☐ Financial problems	Habitual pattern of bad financial decisions
☐ Wrong goals/decisions	Outcome focused on temporal pleasures and material possessions.
☐ Living a lie	Fear that others will discover the hollowness and superficiality of your life
☐ Apathetic	Unconcerned for the feelings or welfare of others

At the conclusion of filling out the strongholds survey go to **appendix B** and list every stronghold symptom in which you placed a number 1 through 10 under **"Your Name"** on the right side of the cross. **** Appendix E, 2.**

Step Two

Renounce the Strongholds

Many have found it helpful to have a witness with them as they renounce the influence of the strongholds. A witness is beneficial not because you need others to help you demolish the strongholds, but **to remind and encourage you** *later when Satan tries to convince you that nothing has changed. If you are married it is appropriate to have your spouse join you in praying through the strongholds that affect you, your marriage, and family. If you are not married or if your spouse is unwilling to help you renounce the stronghold's influence at this time, it's important to find someone close to you with whom to pray.*

Each believer has the power of the Holy Spirit to renounce these strongholds with the authority of the name of Jesus our Lord. We "have divine power to demolish-strongholds" (2 Corinthians 10:4). After you have recognized the symptoms that identify the stronghold, renounce the stronghold and confess any sins that you have committed that relate to its influence. Pray, using the authority of the Name of the Lord Jesus and the power of His shed blood to demolish these strongholds and renounce their influence in your life. Consider the power and authority that Jesus has given His followers as revealed in the following verses.

- *"He appointed twelve — designating them apostles — that they might be with him and that he might send them out to preach and to have* **authority to drive out demons**" *(Mark 3:14,15, emphasis added).*
- *They went out and preached that people should repent. They* **drove out many demons** *and anointed many sick people with oil and healed them" (Mark 6:12,13, emphasis added).*
- *"And these signs will accompany those who believe:* **In my name they will drive out demons**" *(Mark 16:17, emphasis added).*
- *"The seventy-two returned with joy and said,* **'Lord, even the demons submit to us in your name.'** *I have given you* **authority to trample** *on snakes and scorpions and* **to overcome** *all the power of the enemy; nothing will harm you; (Luke 10:17,19, emphasis added).*

Remember that many strongholds hide behind a **veneer of deception**. *As quoted Frangipane earlier, "Once a person is* **deceived**, *he does not* **recognize** *that he is deceived,* **because he has been deceived."** *Lying, fantasies delusions, rationalizations, wrong doctrine, and misuse of Scripture will hinder your arrival at the truth concerning the strongholds that influence and oppress you. I recommend that you* **first renounce the stronghold of deceit.**

Step Three

Cross/essing Thoughts, Feelings, and Attitudes with Writing and Prayer

If you are unsure how to pray, you might consider something like this:

Holy Spirit, please locate the origin of my thought, feeling, and attitude of _____.
I bring it to the cross of Jesus Christ and ask Him to crucify it and put it to death. I renounce the stronghold of _____ By the authority of the name of Jesus Christ according to Your Word. I take back through your power that ground that I surrendered to the enemy and pray that you would fill me with that trust-grounded obedience to Your Holy Spirit so that this area of my life will be in conformity to the image of Christ. In Jesus' Name I pray. Amen.

Father God, I ask your forgiveness of myself for my incorrect perception, forgiveness of every person, place, circumstance, and event which contributed to this thought, feeling, and attitude. With total forgiveness and unconditional love I delete the old, release it, and let it go permanently! In its place I exchange it for _____. By Your grace I choose to put on _____. I allow every physical, mental, emotional, spiritual problem and inappropriate behavior based on the old feeling to quickly disappear. Thank you, Holy Spirit, for coming to my aid and helping me attain the full measure of Your plans and purposes of my creation. Thank you for the deep heart cleansing. In the Mighty Name of Jesus. Amen.

After demolishing the strongholds, remember four important things.

1. Renounce Satanic Thoughts.
- Begin to **take captive every thought to make it obedient to Christ** (See 2 Corinthians 10:5). Do not let the cycle of thoughts, emotions, actions, habits, and strongholds begin again. As you are being harassed, especially by **condemning or critical thoughts, renounce those thoughts** in the name of the Lord Jesus Christ. Don't give Satan a foothold by entertaining demonic spirits.

2. Put on Your Spiritual Armor
- Take back the surrendered ground where strongholds once influenced your life. Choose to put on the spiritual armor that God has given: the **Belt of Truth** – trust in the Lord Jesus, Who declared Himself to be the Truth; the **Breastplate of Righteousness** – assurance that the blood of Christ enables us to stand righteous before the Father; feet fitted with **readiness from the Gospel of Peace** – prepared for His service because He is sanctifying us through and through; the **Shield of Faith** – which by God's power extinguishes the enemy's darts; the **Helmet of Salvation** – which focuses our minds on God and guards against further enemy intrusion; the **Sword of the Spirit** – which we wield as we **immerse ourselves in His Word**; and **Prayer in the Spirit** – that we may be alert and available at all times for communion with God.

Step Three

3. Enlist the Help of Others
- **Seek help** *from your spouse or another believer with whom you have a close relationship. God will use them to help you discern the means He has provided for you to* **meet the seven needs** *He created in us. Otherwise, you may seek a carnal way to meet these needs and provide a foothold for the strongholds to return.*

4. Review the Stronghold List Periodically
- *Go back over the list of strongholds and the accompanying symptoms to see if any* **patterns** *are returning. This last recommendation has been one of the hardest for people to do. Often they will tell us that they have a fear of looking at the stronghold sheet again because of what they might find. But God isn't exposing these strongholds to condemn you. He is seeking you out so that you will* **confess your sins***. Through His forgiveness and cleansing, your* **fellowship with Him** *might once again be restored (see 1 John 1:9).*

After you have exercised the authority of the Name of Jesus to demolish the strongholds, Satan will try to convince you that nothing has happened. But God's Word is true. **We have overcome Satan by the blood of the Lamb and by the word of our testimony!** *Proclaim the victory of the Cross-!*

Refer to the **Cross***-again on* **page 51** *and the* **Put-On / Put-Off chart** *on pages 53 and 54.*

After the influence of the spirits in the strongholds has been renounced by the power and authority of the Lord Jesus Christ, you are able to discern the truths that God wants to reveal to you. The strongholds that were in your soul are replaced by the truth and love that He has wanted to fill you with all along!

Instructions

Place the new spiritual truth on the left side of the Cross **(on page 51-52)** *under the Name of* **"Jesus."**

Meditate on the following verses, putting your name into the verse to **personalize** *the truths in it. Pray for sensitivity to the Holy Spirit's* **prompting** *as He reveals ways in which to* **apply** *the spiritual truth He wishes to develop in you. Some have found it helpful to use the paragraph beneath the verses as a prayer guide.*

Stronghold	**Spiritual Truth**
DECEIT	**SPIRIT OF TRUTH**

"Jesus said, 'If you hold to my teaching, you are really my disciples. Then you will know the truth, and the truth will set you free'"(John 8:31, 32). "Whoever would love life and see good days must keep his tongue from evil and his lips from deceitful speech. He must turn from evil and do good; he must seek peace and pursue it. For the eyes of the Lord are on the righteous and his ears are attentive to their prayer, but the face of the Lord is against those who do evil"(1 Peter 3:10-12).

Because Satan is a liar and the father of lies, he has at his disposal many means of infiltrating the pure truth of the gospel. Paul warned Timothy to stay away from those who engage in godless chatter or quarreling about controversial topics. Recognize that some elements of falsehood may have penetrated your mind, will, and emotions. Renounce the work of Satan in those areas of your life and claim the victory of the blood of Christ as one of His redeemed. Heed Paul's admonition to Timothy, appropriating its truths by the Spirit: "Flee the evil desires of youth, and pursue righteousness, faith, love and peace, along with those who call on the

Lord out of a pure heart"(2 Timothy 2:22). Choose companions whose hearts are also set on loving obedience to God.

Stronghold   *Spiritual Truth*
BITTERNESS   **FORGIVING HEART**

"If you forgive men when they sin against you, your heavenly Father will also forgive you. But if you do not forgive men their sin, your Father will not forgive your sins"(Matthew 6:14,15). "[Love] keeps no record of wrongs"(1 Corinthians 13:5).

Ask God to fill you with the sacrificial love that He demonstrated by sending His Son to lay down His life for you. Pray for those who have mistreated you, remembering that the only One Who can handle vengeance without sinning is God. If you are to walk in the steps of Jesus (see 1 Peter 2:21), if you want to call your Heavenly Father "Abba" (see Romans 8:15-17), you must learn to suffer as He did. This will mean that the hurt you receive from those close to you must be seen from God's vantage point. He caused His own Son to Suffer so that He would learn obedience (see Hebrews 5:8). As a wise friend once told us, "You will never learn to walk in the fullness of Jesus until you can wash the feet of Judas."

Stronghold   *Spiritual Truth*
HEAVINESS   **PRAISE**

"To bestow on them a crown of beauty instead of ashes, the oil of gladness instead of mourning, and a garment of praise instead of a spirit of despair"(Isaiah 61:3). "Praise the Lord, O my soul, and forget not all his benefits, who forgives all your sins and heals all your diseases; who redeems your life from the pit and crowns you with love and compassion"(Psalm 103:2-4).

Take back that ground where the enemy has sown depression, loneliness, self-pity — the "ashes" of hopelessness — and pray for God to plant in you a heart **willing to rejoice** in Him. As you express songs of praise to God for Who He is, He will deliver you from all your fears: "I will extol the Lord at all times; his praise will always be on my lips. My soul will boast in the Lord; let the afflicted hear and rejoice. Glorify the Lord with me; let us exalt his name together. I sought the Lord and he answered me; he delivered me from all my fears"(Psalm 34:1-4). You will receive comfort and strength from the One Who has promised to **be with you always.**

Stronghold   *Spiritual Truth*
JEALOUSY.   **SACRIFICIAL LOVE**

"But since we belong to the day, let us be self-controlled, putting on faith and love as a breastplate, and the hope of salvation as a helmet. Therefore encourage one another and build each other up"(1 Thessalonians 5:8,11). "Love is patient, love is kind. It does not envy, it does not boast, it is not proud. It is not self-seeking, it is not easily angered, and it keeps no record of wrongs. Love does not delight in evil but rejoices with the truth. It always protects, always trusts, always hopes, and always perseveres"(1 Corinthians 13:4-7).

Sacrificial love seeks to benefit others even at a **cost to yourself**: "Do nothing out of selfish ambition or vain conceit, but in humility consider others better than yourselves"(Philippians 2:3). You must choose to turn away from gossip, slander, and godless chatter in order to build one another up. Be sure to examine your inner motives in all you say and do, and ask yourself, **"Would Jesus say or do this?"** Jealousy causes you to delight when a perceived competitor stumbles so that you might then look better. Therefore, God would desire

Step Three

for you to have "a pure heart and a good conscience and a sincere faith" (1 Timothy 1:5) — the qualities of Christ that you need in your soul to take back the surrendered ground of jealousy and distrust.

Stronghold   *Spiritual Truth*
CONFUSION   **FAITH**
(DOUBT AND UNBELIEF)

"Do you not know? Have you not heard? The Lord is the everlasting God, the Creator of the ends of the earth. He will not grow tired or weary, and his understanding no one can fathom. He gives strength to the weary and increases the power of the weak" (Isaiah 40:28,29). "To those who through the righteousness of our God and Savior Jesus Christ have received a faith as precious as ours: Grace and peace be yours in abundance through the knowledge of God and of Jesus our Lord. His divine power has given us everything we need for life and godliness through our knowledge of Him who called us by his own glory and goodness" (2 Peter 1:2,3).

Meditate on the above verses, focusing on the **righteousness of Christ** and **His divine power.** God who is your Creator knows your every fiber. He understands when you are weary and weak. He is the One Who sustains you when you feel lost and downcast. Reclaim that ground the enemy built upon by praying for "the spirit of wisdom and revelation, so that you may know him better" (Ephesians 1:17). Earnestly **seek Him** in the Word and be encouraged by the lives He continues to change around you. **Meditate** on the faith of your spiritual forefathers in Hebrews 11. **Pray** often throughout the day for His will to fulfill that **life and godliness** He has given you.

Stronghold   *Spiritual Truth*
REJECTION   **ACCEPTANCE**

"Praise be to the God and Father of our Lord Jesus Christ! In his great mercy he has given us new birth into a living hope through the resurrection of Jesus Christ from the dead, and into an inheritance that can never perish, spoil or fade — kept in heaven for you, who through faith are shielded by God's power until the coming of the salvation that is ready to be revealed in the last time" (1 Peter 1:3-5). "But you are a chosen people, a royal priesthood, a holy nation, a people belonging to God, that you may declare the praises of him who called you out of darkness into his wonderful light" (1 Peter 2:9).

How could you be any more acceptable to God, Who has declared you to be **His own treasure**, empowered by His Spirit to declare His praise! Praise God for this irrevocable truth. You have great purpose and meaning to God. His commands to His people Israel apply to you as well: "To love the Lord your God, to walk in all his ways, to obey his commands, to hold fast to him and to serve him with all your heart and all your soul" (Joshua 22:5). Pray for Him to reveal the **specific means** for you to enact these commands, step by step, and fill you with joy as you realize how precious you are to Him. You have been purchased by His Son's blood and are His very own!

Stronghold   *Spiritual Truth*
PRIDE   *HUMILITY*

"Clothe yourselves with humility toward one another, because, 'God opposes the proud but gives grace to the humble.' Humble yourselves, therefore, under God's mighty hand, that he may lift you up in due time" (1 Peter 5:5-6). "Be completely humble and gentle; be patient, bearing with one another in love" (Ephesians 4:2). "This is the one I esteem: he who is humble and contrite in spirit, and trembles at my Word" (Isaiah 66:2).

Always remember to thank God for the grace that He has promised to you as you **humble yourself** *before His Lordship! See yourself as a* **servant to others**, *as though you were serving Christ Himself. Be sure that your heart attitude is* **pure**. *If ulterior motives for personal gain or recognition are there, repent and appropriate God's forgiveness and cleansing (see 1 John 1:9). Pray that God will provide* **opportunities for spiritual fruit** *— love, joy, peace, patience, kindness, goodness, faithfulness, gentleness, self-control — to be manifested as you put others ahead of yourself.*

Stronghold	*Spiritual Truth*
RELIGIOSITY	**PRAISE AND PEACE**

"Love the Lord your God with all your heart and with all your soul and with all your strength and with all your mind' and, 'Love your neighbor as yourself.' 'You have answered correctly,' Jesus replied. 'Do this and you will live'" (Luke 10:27,28). "This is what the Sovereign Lord, the Holy One of Israel, says: 'In repentance and rest is your salvation, in quietness and trust is your strength, but you would have none of it'" (Isaiah 30:15).

Set aside for yourself a **sabbatical** *from church-related activities. Spend time quietly before God; ask Him to reveal to you different facets of Who He is. Ponder in the Word the different* **names of God** *and their implications for your life, e.g., the Prince of Peace, the Alpha and Omega, etc. Allow the Spirit to well up within you a heart of praise for God. Ask Him to open your eyes to opportunities to serve Him by serving others* **as He reveals them**. *Resist attempts by well-meaning friends to get you back into the "old groove" unless God makes it clear that He is the one opening each door.* **Be accountable** *to your spouse or intimate circle of friends to move at the impulse of His love and not out of guilt or performance motivation.*

Stronghold	*Spiritual Truth*
INDEPENDENCE	**UNITY AND COMMITMENT**
and DIVORCE	

"May the God who gives endurance and encouragement give you a spirit of unity among yourselves as you follow Christ Jesus, so that with one heart and mouth you may glorify the God and Father of our Lord Jesus Christ. Accept one another, then, just as Christ accepted you, in order to bring praise to God." (Romans 15:5-7). "Just as each of us has one body with many members, and these members do not all have the same function, so in Christ we who are many form one body, and each member belongs to all the others" (Romans 12:4,5).

Followers of Christ are each baptized by the Spirit into one body (see 1 Corinthians 12:13). Proclaim this truth to your inner being: God has combined the members of the body so that there should be no division but that the parts **should have equal concern for each other**. *With the spiritual gifts God has given to his body, you are to bring glory to Him by serving one another and the world. Will the world come to Christ if they do not see how Christians love and are committed to one another? Whether in a marriage, a family, a faith community or the workplace, pray for the will and the desire to* **join with God** *in the purpose He has for your life in conjunction with others. Ask for "spiritual eyes and ears" to recognize and understand your part in the Kingdom of God. Pray for the Spirit to pour into you a desire and understanding to be "joined and held together by every supporting ligament" in a faith body that is growing and building itself up in love as each part does its work (see Ephesians 4:16).*

Step Three

Stronghold	*Spiritual Truth*
STUPOR and PRAYERLESSNESS	*PERSEVERANCE AND HOPE*

"Therefore, since we have a great high priest who has gone through the heavens, Jesus the Son of God, let us hold firmly to the faith we profess. For we do not have a high priest who is unable to sympathize with our weaknesses, but we have one who has been tempted in every way, just as we are —yet was without sin. Let us then approach the throne of grace with confidence, so that we also rejoice in our sufferings, because we know that suffering produces perseverance; perseverance, character; and character, hope. And hope does not disappoint us, because God has poured out his love into our hearts by the Holy Spirit, whom he has given us" *(Romans 5:2-5).*

Satan will often use two tactics to keep you from drawing near to God through prayer: (1) He may cause you to misperceive God's work of developing hope in you. God's plan is to use **suffering** to produce perseverance, character, and finally **hope** in you. As you suffer, Satan may convince you that your suffering is a sign of God's rejection. A coldness and distance toward God may enter your relationship with Him. (2) Even after you have confessed your sins and they are forgiven, Satan may use **"false guilt"** to keep you from approaching God. He will remind you of what you have done and also attempt to convince you that you must earn back God's love. The truth of the matter is that the sacrificial shed blood of Jesus enables you to **approach God** in your time of need. When you are feeling distant from God, ask the Holy Spirit to help you. Your faith must be unshakable in knowing that God does use suffering to develop in you the **character of Jesus**. Have **confidence** in your position in Christ as you draw near to your Heavenly Father.

Stronghold	*Spiritual Truth*
REBELLION	*FEAR OF THE LORD*

"Therefore, since we are receiving a kingdom that cannot be shaken, let us be thankful, and so worship God acceptably with reverence and awe, for our God is a consuming fire" *(Hebrews 12:28-29).* "The Lord is near to all who call on him, to all who call on him in truth. He fulfills the desires of those who fear him; he hears their cry and saves them"*(Psalm 145:18-19).*

Pray that the Holy Spirit will restore in you an **awesome respect** of God's power and Person: God is "the King eternal, immortal, invisible, the only God" *(see 1 Timothy 1:17).* Ask that the blind areas of your mind that has rebelled as Satan did to "be like God" *(see Genesis 3:5),* would instead "see the light of the gospel of the glory of Christ, who is the image of God" *(2 Corinthians 4:4).* **Stand firm** in recognizing the tempter's wiles to lure you away from the awe and reverence due our holy God, and search the Scriptures daily to reinforce a constant gratefulness of **Who He is** and who you are.

Stronghold	*Spiritual Truth*
FEAR AND INSECURITY	*COURAGE, FAITH, AND TRUST*

"The Lord is with me; I will not be afraid. What can man do to me? The Lord is with me; he is my helper. I will look in triumph on my enemies. It is better to take refuge in the Lord than to trust in man"*(Psalm 118:6-9).* "Do not fear, for I am with you; do not be dismayed, for I am your God. I will strengthen you and help you, I will uphold you with my righteous right hand"*(Isaiah 41:10).* "Peace I leave with you; my peace I give you. I do not give to you as the world gives. Do not let your hearts be troubled and do not be afraid"*(John 14:27).*

*Agitation from the devil blocks your absolute trust and faith in the Lordship of Christ in your life and makes you feel as if all responsibilities and decisions rest on you alone. Prayerfully relinquish all goals, activities, and outcomes into God's hands, recognizing that His goals for you are **joyful obedience** to Him and the **development of Christ-likeness** as you interact with others. Begin to recognize the people He has placed in your life as **instruments of refinement** for your character. Pray that God will develop spiritual fruit in you as you choose to value individuals more highly than tasks. As you pray for the Holy Spirit to breathe into you an overwhelming sense of "holy boldness" for the sake of Jesus, you will take your eyes off your perceived inadequacies and focus on being a **faithful servant** of God. You can cast all of your worries and anxieties on God, firmly believing that He cares for you (see 1 Peter 5:7). And if you suffer for doing what is right, you can be assured that the "Spirit of glory" will rest on you!*

Stronghold   Spiritual Truth
CONTROL   SUBMISSION AND YIELDEDNESS

"Submit to one another out of reverence for Christ" (Ephesians 5:21). "'God opposes the proud but gives grace to the humble.' Submit yourselves, then, to God" (James 4:6,7). "He guides the humble in what is right and teaches them his way" (Psalm 25:9).

God is seeking to work in you the fruit of a **gentle and reverent spirit**, which cannot coexist with a striving and manipulative one. As you yield control of your circumstances and relationships to Him, by His grace He will replace worry with trust, insensitivity with car for others, desire for recognition with a humble and contrite heart. Pray for opportunities to become an encouraging **"fan"** of others, helping them to succeed.

Stronghold   Spiritual Truth
SEXUAL.   HOLINESS

"Since everything will be destroyed in this way, what kind of people ought you to be? You ought to live holy and godly lives as you look forward to the day of God and speed its coming...Make every effort to be found spotless, blameless and at peace with him" (2 Peter 3:11-14). "As obedient children, do not conform to the evil desires you had when you lived in ignorance. But just as he who called you is holy, so be holy in all you do; for it is written: 'Be holy, because I am holy'" (1 Peter 1:14-16).

God is holy and He requires **holiness** in His people. Sexual impurity blocks the virtue of God to guide our lives: "Without holiness no one will see the Lord" (Hebrews 12:14). Satan knows this truth. He also knows the final judgment outcome of people who continue to live in sexual immorality. Eliminate from your life **all agents of temptation**: magazines, pictures, movies, tapes, TV — anything that can help plant a foothold in your mind. Only the Holy Spirit can help you to resist and overcome these temptations, and, through grace, draw you near to the heart of Jesus. Submit to God and **resist temptation by praying**; ask for His protection and cling to the Lord of Righteousness in trusting faith.

Stronghold   Spiritual Truth
IDOLATRY   LORDSHIP OF CHRIST

"Since, then, you have been raised with Christ, set your hearts on things above, where Christ is seated at the right hand of God. Set your minds on things above, not on earthly things. For you died, and your life is now hidden with Christ in God" (Colossians 3:1-3). "I do not write to you because you do not know the truth, but because you do know it and because no lie comes from the truth. See that what you have heard from the beginning remains in you. If it does, you also will remain in the Son and in the Father. And this is what he promised us — even eternal life"(1 John 2:21, 24, 25).

Remember: The early Church understood that when a person was **"born again"** it meant that he had put his **full trust and reliance** in the Lord Jesus.

When you have finished praising and thanking the Father for who you now are in Christ (2 Corinthians 5:17), you are ready to complete the Cross/essing. Take a red pen or pencil and mark out "Your Name" with an X. Place your name next to Jesus' Name. Put a big X through all strongholds listed on the right side of the Cross. Put Jesus' name in place of yours. (See scriptures on the Cross, **page 55**). As you do this exercise meditate on this Scripture: **"I have been crucified with Christ; It is no longer I who live, but Christ lives in me; and the life I now live in the flesh I live by faith in the Son of God, who loved me and gave Himself for me." (Galatians 2:20-21).**

Your Identity In Christ

*Because of Christ redemption you are a new creation of infinite worth. You are deeply loved, completely forgiven, you are fully pleasing, you are totally accepted by God, you are absolutely complete in Christ. When your performance reflects your new identity in Christ that reflection is dynamically unique. There has never been another person like you in the history of mankind, nor will there ever be. God has made you an original one of a kind, really somebody. ******** Appendix. E, 8.*

Appendix

Table of Contents

TITLE	PAGE
A. I Wear a Thousand Masks	51
B. Cross/essing	53
C. Put on - Put off chart	55
D. Scriptures on the Cross	57
E. Resources taken from:	59

CHARTS

F. Lake of Blessings Chart	60
G. A Heart of Flesh for A Heart of Stone	61

Appendix A

I Wear a Thousand Masks

I hope you won't be fooled by me for I wear a mask. I wear a thousand masks, that
I'm afraid to take off, and none of them is me.

I am likely to give you the impression that I'm secure, that confidence is my name and
coolness my game, that the water is calm and I'm in command, and that I need no one.
But I hope you won't believe me.

My surface may seem smooth…beneath I dwell in confusion, in fear, in aloneness.
But I hide this. I panic at the thought of my weakness and fear being exposed.
That's why I frantically create a mask to hide behind.

If I don't keep the mask in front of myself I am afraid you'll think less of me,
you'll laugh, and your laugh will kill me.

So I play my game, with a facade of self-assurance without and a trembling feeling within.
And my life becomes a front. I idly chatter to you in suave tones. So when I go through my routine,
I hope you won't be fooled by what I'm saying. I hope you hear what I'm not saying.

I dislike the superficial phony game I'm playing. I'd really like to be open, genuine and spontaneous.
I want your help in doing this. I want you to risk approaching me even when it seems as if that's
the last thing I want or need. I want this from you so that I'll be alive. Each time you're kind,
and gentle and encouraging, each time you try to understand because you really care,
my courage to risk sharing myself with you increases.

I want you to know how important you are to me. How you can help me reshape the person
that is me if you choose. But it will not be easy for you. A long conviction of
worthlessness leads me to maintain distance.

The nearer you approach me, the blinder I may strike back. It is self-defeating but at the time
it seems the safest thing to do. I fight against the very things that I cry out for. My long conviction of
worthlessness builds strong walls. But I am told that love is stronger than the strongest walls and in
this lies hope. I desperately want you to understand me in spite of my distancing tactics.

Who am I, you may wonder? I am someone you know very well. I am every man and woman you meet.

Author unknown

Appendix B

CROSS
KNOW WHO WE ARE IN CHRIST
　Understand what Jesus did for you at the cross.
　** Appendix E, 2.

Jesus	Your name
Holy	
Pure	
Perfect	
Righteous	
Truth	
Loving	
Patient	
Kind	
Forgiveness	
Godly	
Eternal	
Servant	
Selfless	
Merciful	
Sinless	

Appendix B

Appendix B *(continued)*

Appendix C

"PUT ON - PUT OFF"

"...Lay aside every weight, and ...sin." Hebrews 12:1-2
***********Appendix E, 11.

PUT OFF	Scriptural Insight	PUT ON	Scriptural Insight
1. Lacking of Love	1 John 4:7-8, 20	Love	John 15:12
2. Judging	Matt. 7:1-2	Self-examination	John 8:9; 15:22
3. Bitterness	Heb. 12:15	Tenderhearted	Col. 3:12
4. Unforgiving Spirit	Mark 11:26	Forgiving Spirit	Matt. 6:14
5. Pride	Proverbs 16:18	Humility	James 4:6
6. Selfishness	Phil. 2:21	Death of Self	John 12:24
7. Boasting (conceit)	1 Cor. 4:7	Humility	Proverbs 27:2
8. Stubbornness	1 Sam. 15:23	Submission	Romans 6:13
9. Lack of Submission or Disrespect	2 Tim. 3:6	Broken Will	Matt. 6:10
10. Rebellion	1 Sam. 15:23	Submitting - Jesus, Lord	Joel 2:12-13
11. Disobedience	1 Sam. 12:15	Obedience	Heb. 5:9
12. Ungratefulness	Romans 1:21	Thankfulness	Eph. 5:20
13. Impatience	James 1:2-4	Patience	Luke 21:19
14. Discontent	Phil. 4:11-13	Satisfaction	Heb. 13:5
15. Covetousness	Exodus 20:17	Yielding Rights	Col. 3:5
16. Murmuring	Proverbs 19:3	Gratefulness	1 Cor. 10:10
17. Complaining	Jude 15-16	Contentment	Heb. 13:5-6
18. Sassing	John 6:43	Respect for Authority	Eph. 5:21
19. Irritation to Others	Proverbs 25:8	Preferring in Love	Phil. 2:3-4
20. Jealousy	Proverbs 27:4	Trust, preferring others	1 Cor. 13:4

Appendix C

PUT OFF	Scriptural Insight	PUT ON	Scriptural Insight
21. Strife	James 3:16	Esteem of others	Luke 6:31
22. Losing temper	Proverbs 16:32	Self-control	Romans 5:3-4
23. Bodily harm	Proverbs 16:29	Gentleness	1 Thess. 2:7
24. Anger	Proverbs 14:17	Self-control	Gal. 5:24-25
25. Wrath	James 1:19-20	Self-control	Gal. 5:24-25
26. Hatred	Matt. 5:21-22	Love or kindness	1 Cor. 13:3
27. Murder	Exodus 20:13	Love	Romans 13:10
28. Gossip	1 Tim. 5:13	Speaking with praise	Romans 14:19
29. Lying	Eph. 4:25	Speaking truth	Zech. 8:16
30. Bad language	Eph. 4:29	Edification	1 Tim. 4:12
31. Profanity	Psalm 109:17	Edification	1 Tim. 4:12
32. Idle words	Matt. 12:36	Bridle the tongue	Proverbs 21:23
33. Evil thoughts	Proverbs 23:7a	"Think on these things"	Phil. 4:8
34. Bad motives	1 Sam. 16:7	Meditation on God	Psalm 19:14
35. Complacency	James 4:17	Diligence	Col. 3:23
36. Hypocrisy	Job 8:13	Honesty	Eph. 4:25
37. Other gods	Deut. 11:16	Jesus 1st Place	Eph. 4:6
38. Lost first love	Revelation 2:4	Meditate on Christ	1 John 4:10, 19
39. Lack of rejoicing	Phil. 4:4	Rejoicing	1 Thess. 5:16
40. Worry (fear)	Matt. 6:25-32	Trust	1 Peter 5:7
41. Doubt (unbelief)	1 Thess. 5:24	Faith	Heb. 11:1

Appendix D

Scriptures on the Cross

2 Corinthians 5:21 For He made Him who knew no sin to be sin for us that we might become the righteousness of God in Him.

1 Peter 2:24 Who Himself bore our sins in His own body on the tree, that we, having died to sins, might live for righteousness—by whose stripes you were healed.

1 John 3:5 And you know that He was manifested to take away our sins, and in Him there is not sin.

Psalm 32:5-7 Then I acknowledged my sin to You, and did not cover my iniquity (completely unfolding the past until all is revealed). "I will confess my transgressions to the Lord" and You (instantly) forgave the guilt of my sin. Therefore let everyone who is godly pray to You while you may be found: Surely when the waters rise, they will not reach him. You are my hiding place; You will protect me from trouble; And surround me with songs of deliverance. **Selah**

Galatians 2:20-21 I have been crucified with Christ; it is no longer I who live, but Christ lives in me; and the life I now live in the flesh I live by faith in the Son of God, who loved me and gave Himself for me.

1 Corinthians 1:30 But of Him you are in Christ Jesus, who became for us wisdom from God—and righteousness and sanctification and redemption—that, as it is written, "He that glories, let him glory in the Lord."

Colossians 1:27 ....."Christ in you the hope of glory

Appendix E

Resources Taken From:

1. Rick Warren. The Purpose Driven Life. *

2. Dick & Judy French. M.O.R.E. Ministry of Reconciliation & Encouragement. **

3. Mike and Sue Dowgiewicz. Restoration Ministries International. ***

4. Liberty Savard. Breaking The Power. ****

5. Beth Moore. Breaking Free. *****

6. Fred Littauer. The Promise of Restoration. Breaking the bands of Emotional Bondage. ******

7. Paula Sandford. Healing Victims of Sexual Abuse. *******

8. Robert McGee. The Search For Significance. Page 58. ********

9. Graphics by In His Image Sharon http://www.hisimage.org See Cover design. *********

10. John and Paula Sanford. God's Lake of Blessing. Page 57.

11. H. Norman Wright. Put-Off Put-On Chart. Pages 53 & 54.

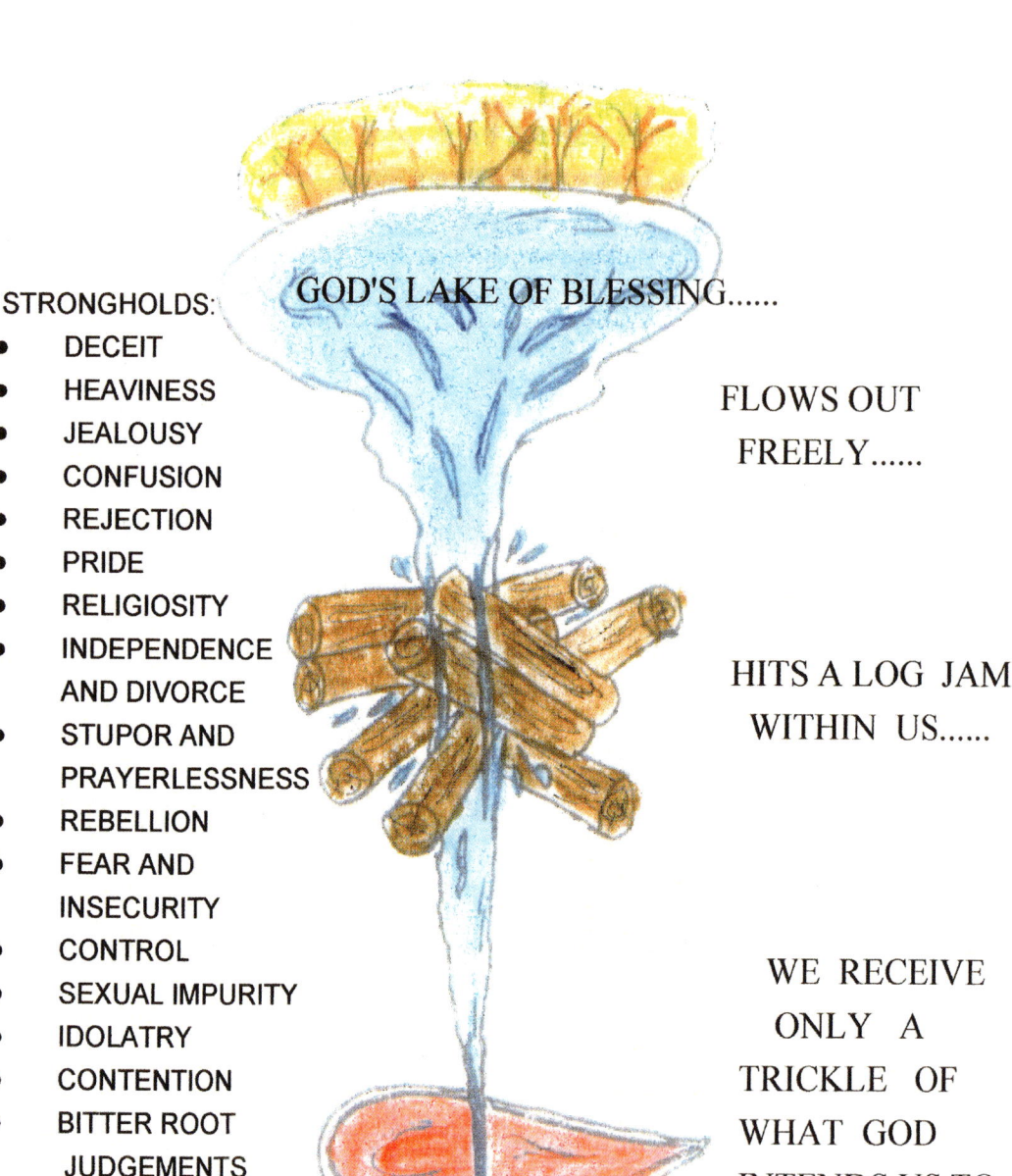

GOD'S LAKE OF BLESSING......

STRONGHOLDS:
- DECEIT
- HEAVINESS
- JEALOUSY
- CONFUSION
- REJECTION
- PRIDE
- RELIGIOSITY
- INDEPENDENCE AND DIVORCE
- STUPOR AND PRAYERLESSNESS
- REBELLION
- FEAR AND INSECURITY
- CONTROL
- SEXUAL IMPURITY
- IDOLATRY
- CONTENTION
- BITTER ROOT JUDGEMENTS
- INNER VOWS
- HEARTS OF STONE
- LIES

FLOWS OUT FREELY......

HITS A LOG JAM WITHIN US......

WE RECEIVE ONLY A TRICKLE OF WHAT GOD INTENDS US TO HAVE.......

Strongholds are *sinful self protections.* However, they usually get us the thing we *fear*. They are *mental, spiritual, and emotional* structures (such as bitter root judgement, lies, inner vows, hearts of stone), we *unknowingly build protecting ourselves*. Therefore, the rewards of strongholds are SEEMING *protection, power, control, and security.* However they keep *God* out. They keep *truth* out. They become so much a part of us they SEEM like us. ***********Appendix E, 10.*

A HEART OF FLESH FOR A HEART OF STONE

A new heart will I give you, and a new spirit will I put within you: and I will take away the stony heart out of your flesh and give you a <u>heart of flesh.</u> And I will put my Spirit within you and cause you to walk in My statutes, and you shall heed My ordinances, and do them.   (Ezekiel 36: 26,27)

Fruits Of The Spirit:
Love,
Joy,
Peace,
Goodness,
Self-control,
Meekness,
Patience,
Kindness,
Faithfulness,
Truthfulness

Romans 8:15
Spirit of Adoption vs
Spirit of Slavery....

Heart of Flesh	Heart of Stone
Flexible	Tightened
Soft	Hard
Open	Closed
Wise	Ignorant
Humility	Arrogance
Meekness	Pride
Self-control	Self-centered
Gentle	Haughty
Forebearing	Alienated
Caring	Indifferent
Good	Mean
Obedient	Disobedient
Self-Validated	Self-conceited
Complimentary	Competative
Encouraging	Provoking
Peaceful	Irritated
Rejoicing	Envying
Honoring	Jealous
Holy	Wicked

Deliverance Definition:
The process of being released and set free to live and embrace life in all its facets; spontaenously, systematically, and purposefully, without the hindrances of fear, torment, darkness, and unbelief.   Judy French   ** *Appendix E, 2.*

Isaiah 61:1 He has sent me to heal the brokenhearted, and to proclaim liberty to the physical and spiritual captives and the opening of the prison and of the eyes of those who are bound.

Made in the USA
Charleston, SC
13 September 2013